Reaching a RELUCTANT GENERATION

Engaging the Culture with the Message of Jesus

DARRIN VAUGHAN

Reaching a Reluctant Generation
by Darrin Vaughan

Printed in the United States of America

ISBN 978-0692025017

E-mail: info@darrinvaughan.com
Website: darrinvaughan.com

Dedication

I dedicate this book to my best friend and the love of my life, Eva. She has stood beside me for the past eight years of marriage. She has taught me to be courageous in the face of doubt and to believe God during tough times. You are an amazing wife and the kindest person I know.

Table of Contents

Introduction

Within recent years, there has been a seemingly insurmountable tidal wave of indifference that has hit our culture. It threatens to unravel the spiritual fabric of our society. With increasing reluctance in adhering to church tradition or aligning with a particular denomination, this generation of believers is rapidly exiting mainstream Christianity. In an attempt to modernize their way of thinking, they have adopted a low view of church and a low view of God. Unfortunately, this way of thinking has diluted the Gospel, and has hindered countless millions from being transformed by an unconditionally loving God.

The greatest need of our generation is for ordinary men and women to be infused with a burning love for Jesus.

The greatest need of our generation is for ordinary men and women to be infused with a burning love for Jesus that motivates them to present people with the matchless message of the cross. This message has been polluted, distorted, and ultimately filtered down to the point that it fails to produce the results of the first-century church. I have written this book for the purpose of awakening your hearts to the reality of humanity's separation from God and to empower you to answer His call to be a voice in your communities.

We have to begin thinking on a larger scale, which starts in the most unassuming places—by reaching out to our own families and neighbors. If we remain silent now, a whole generation could slip through the cracks and the blame would be on us. We have all heard the disheartening statistics. Many professing Christians have never even shared their faith with an unbeliever.

Do not misunderstand me; I am not making a blanket statement about the entirety of the church. I am referring to those who choose to ignore the countless masses of people who need to be confronted with their own mortality. It is to our shame that we have become more inward focused than outward.

As far as this life is concerned, we will all die, but many are facing a second death far worse than any "hell on earth." It is to this end that we labor in the fields that are "white for harvest." Could you imagine what would happen if our churches invested more money in evangelism than any other program? It would result in another Great Awakening!!!

Acts 2:1-4 (ESV),

The Coming of the Holy Spirit

1 When the day of Pentecost arrived, they were all
together in one place. 2 And suddenly there came from
heaven a sound like a mighty rushing wind, and it filled
the entire house where they were sitting. 3 And divided
tongues as of fire appeared to them and rested on each
one of them. 4 And they were all filled with the Holy
Spirit and began to speak in other tongues as the Spirit
gave them utterance.

These verses are the proof that God never intended for us to do evangelism alone. Through the Holy Spirit, God gave us a far better agent of change than any amount of clever programming we could ever hope to muster up. This experience makes us "partakers of the divine nature" (2 Peter 1:4).

It was at the cross that Jesus purchased the church with His blood, and it is at the cross that sinful men become saints; but it was in the upper room where the saints became His burning ones.

We have been branded by the Holy Spirit so that God could "make His minister's a flame of fire" (Hebrews 1:7). With this new encounter, spiritual fervor replaced lifeless religious liturgy. It's time for us to trade going through the motions with undivided devotion. God is on a mission to find His lost "Adams" and reintroduce them to "The Tree of Life."

Do you remember how you felt the day you honestly committed your life to Jesus? If you were anything like me you probably felt apprehension, mixed with a newfound excitement. I burned inside with a burden to reach the lost. It was as if God instantly began to download into my heart His passion to reach souls.

I remember asking a person who attended that night's meeting, "What do I do now?" He told me to go back to my church, get some Gospel tracts, and begin handing them out. I didn't even know what a Gospel tract was; I was just so overwhelmed by God's presence that I needed to tell someone. I went to my pastor, told him what happened, and asked him if he had anything I could give out to people. He was probably more pumped than I was about my recent news. Pastors love to see members of their church get excited about evangelism.

That night I went to our local fair and witnessed to everyone I had been intimidated to share my faith with. I had lived my high school years as a "poser Christian." I was one of the biggest hypocrites I knew, but God set me on a new path and His Word has been my compass since 1999. I've never been the same since.

The early church thrived because ordinary men and women burned with a fresh message of their life-changing encounter with Jesus. They refused to be silent, even through one of the most intense times of persecution the church has ever faced. The harder the world's system tried to eradicate this message, the more it grew.

We must be ignited with a passion for the lost just like the early church was. They didn't have a New Testament; they *were* the New Testament. The one thing they did have was a new testimony. If Jesus has saved you, healed you, forgiven you, and restored you, then you have a message that someone needs to hear.

For those of you who have set your affections on the Lord and have surrendered yourself unreservedly to His every desire for your life, you will inevitably experience the cruel skepticism of the lukewarm and indifferent. They will taunt and undermine your efforts to pursue God, but their chidings must not stop your progress. They are those cold, timid souls who have remained unmoved by the Holy Spirit's pleadings to bring them to completion in Christ.

If Jesus has saved you, healed you, forgiven you, and restored you, then you have a message that someone needs to hear.

For some reason they have been stifled in their own pursuit of God and now feel it is their mission to stifle everyone else who has surpassed their current position. You must not listen to their words, for they are like poison to your soul. You must not imitate their lifestyle, lest you become like them. Paul said, "Follow me as I follow Christ" (1 Corinthians 11:1).

The devil is really good at playing on our emotions. He always presents us with the worst possible scenario. Like a never-ending tape recorder, he fuels our fears with vain imaginations because he knows if we believe his lies then we will forsake the Great Commission.

Satan wants us to waste our lives spinning our wheels, doing "religious activities" that eventually rob us of the joy of being a soul winner. He wants you to believe that witnessing to people isn't what God has called you to do. We then come up with our best excuses: "Let the evangelist do it. Let the pastor do it. Let the extravert do it. I'm not qualified. I haven't had sufficient training. I would be better suited for something a little less confrontational; something behind the scenes." The problem with this thinking, as rational as it may sound, is that it cannot be backed up by Scripture.

The question He's asking you and me today is, "Will you burn for Me, even if you're the only one burning?"

Our mission in life is to follow Christ. We must fix our eyes on Him—not on other people. The best of men will fail, but God has never failed. He wants to set you aside for His own special purposes and cause you to "so shine before men."

The question He's asking you and me today is, "Will you burn for Me, even if you're the only one burning?" If you answered yes, then prepare yourself to be amazed by what God will do through an ordinary person (YOU)!

Chapter 1

Where Have My Disciples Gone?

If you listen closely you will hear the voice of Jesus calling out to His misplaced disciples, "Where are you?" Every Sunday we go to our churches and sit in the pews next to people who are silently struggling through life. Some have been hurt and scarred to the point of complete despondency to the Lord. Others have lost their passion for Jesus and exchanged it for lifeless gods. They put on a nice, smiling face, but are really empty inside.

These are the misplaced disciples. They once burned bright for the Lord, but now the fire has gone out and only a smoldering wick remains. They go through the motions and talk about the "good ol' days," with no intention of changing.

These are the misplaced disciples. They once burned bright for the Lord, but now the fire has gone out and only a smoldering wick remains.

I have had the opportunity to minister in many different denominations and meet a vast array of different people. I have seen the effects poor leadership and religious manipulation have on the psyche of a congregation. Sometimes the greatest threat to a member of a church is in the church itself.

I remember preaching at a small church in Alabama. It became clear to me within the first five minutes of my arrival that something was a bit strange about the behavior of the congregation. No sooner had I stepped through the front door than a woman approached me with a long list of names of those who were sick in the church. I could tell by looking at the size of the congregation there were more people on her list than were in attendance.

The red flags continued through the night. The choir robes were dated, the church was stuffy, and there was little organization. At one point, a man fell asleep while I was ministering. It appeared as if the church was on its last leg. I was almost done speaking when I noticed a glimmer of hope. There was a lady about three rows back, sitting by her husband, who began to weep.

Finally, after about an hour of little emotion, someone was getting their breakthrough. I began speaking into her life. I expected her husband to give some kind of support, but he never once looked up or stretched out his hand to pray for her.

This church did not have a pastor or good leaders to help guide them. I sensed they had given up, not realizing the life God intended for them. Unfortunately the church was shut down shortly after my visit.

Revival is always preceded by repentance and spiritual hunger.

I wonder what would have happened if that man would have taken interest in the well-being of his wife. He could have been the key to open the doors of revival, but because of an unwillingness to yield to the Holy Spirit the whole church suffered. Revival is always preceded by repentance and spiritual hunger. Where these qualities are absent there will also be an absence of the presence of God.

Lukewarm believers stifle a move of God through their brazen resistance to His Spirit and indifference to His holiness. A lifestyle of rebellion is a process that does not take place overnight. It usually creeps in unaware and takes time to evolve. Remember, the devil is a thief. Thieves do not come through the front door. They cowardly crawl through the back window. Satan has never worked harder than he did the hours leading up to the death of Jesus. He crawled through a back window left open by Judas. Once inside he was able to poison the hearts of the disciples.

Jesus already knew they would fall away that night, even though each of them declared it would never happen. Mark 14:27, "Then Jesus said to them, 'All of you will be made to stumble because of Me this night, for it is written: "I will strike the Shepherd, And the sheep will be scattered."'"

We all talk about the terrible crime of Judas, selling Jesus out to the Pharisees and religious rulers for a few pieces of silver. We have to wonder how close the other disciples were from turning on Jesus. And for that matter, how many times have we exchanged His glory for something worthless?

Jesus said in Matthew 16:26, "For what is a man profited, if he shall gain the whole world, and lose his own soul? Or what shall a man give in exchange for his soul?"

How much would you be willing to sell Jesus out for? I bet if we were honest with ourselves the answer would shock us. We fail to realize how easy it is to make something other than Jesus our object of worship. We need to allow the Holy Spirit into the deep and hidden places of our heart to uncover any secret sins.

Aren't you glad that the One who deserves to be pursued comes and pursues us, even after we have sinned *royally*? Just like with His disciples, He knows our weaknesses and He knows if and when we will mess up.

Called Out

Imagine God's eyes spanning the universe, searching for those who would become His disciples. Well, you don't have to imagine, because that is what He is doing. He is calling to those disciples already accounted for, to present His love to the unlovely and His passion to the passionless.

Several years ago I attended a discipleship program in Alabama called Master's Commission. We traveled all over the United States ministering in schools and churches. We did everything from street preaching to pulpit ministry. What I learned during that one year was priceless.

The following year I went on staff with Master's Commission as an evangelist. I wrote a booklet and distributed it to several pastors in an attempt to secure speaking engagements. None of my efforts seemed to pan out and soon discouragement set in.

One day I was praying outside behind the church I attended at the time. As I was crying out to God for direction, I noticed two young men walking down the alley just opposite of the church. I felt impressed to speak to them, but at first declined God's prompting because I was too consumed with my own problems. The urging from the Holy Spirit grew stronger and I realized I would be in direct disobedience to God if I did not talk to them.

After having shuffled my feet for some time, the guys had already made it across a huge field. I yelled to them, but they did not pay attention to me. I ran and jumped in my car, praying the whole way for God to give me a specific word to speak to them. I parked my car at a gas station near where I saw them walking, and quickly made my way down the street.

When I finally approached them, the words to speak came to me. I said, "God wanted me to tell you that He loves you." I know this seems like a generic statement, but it opened the door to the ensuing conversation. One of the guys said, "You would never believe what somebody texted me today. The text said, 'God loves you.'"

From there I preached the Word of the Lord boldly to these two guys. It seemed as if the words poured forth from my mouth, divinely orchestrated by heaven. The Word pierced into their hearts and conviction drew them to a place of repentance.

One of the men began to weep uncontrollably, so I asked them if they were saved. They said no, so I prayed for them to receive salvation. I then asked them if they had ever heard of the Holy Spirit. They said no, so I explained who He was, and that He desired relationship with us. I asked them if I could pray with them so that His presence would be made real to them. As I prayed one of the men began to shake and fell to the ground, speaking in other tongues. Notice I did not tell them to speak in tongues or to shake. I knew this experience was authentic since they professed no previous knowledge of the Holy Spirit.

God has called us to reach the people that everyone else has forgotten.

I left amazed and dumbfounded at what God just did. My paradigm of Him changed that day.

God has called us to reach the people that everyone else has forgotten. These are His diamonds in the rough. He is ready to excavate them out of the pit they are in and showcase them to the world.

What About Peter?

Peter was one of these diamonds, but where had he gone after Jesus died? Surely he would not deny His Lord. Let's not forget that it was Peter who walked on water with Jesus, and it was Peter who was on the Mount of Transfiguration with Him; it was also Peter who declared Him to be the Christ, the Son of the Living God. Surely, he would have been an example for the rest of the disciples to follow.

Before Jesus was crucified He spoke two very alarming prophecies to Peter. In the first prophecy, Jesus told Peter that he would deny Him three different times. Of course, Peter denied the fact that he was going to deny Jesus. How many times have we ignored the rebuke of the Lord? Remember what Scripture says in Hebrews 12:5-6,

> 5 And you have forgotten the exhortation which speaks to you as to sons: "My son, do not despise the chastening of the Lord, Nor be discouraged when you are rebuked by Him; 6 For whom the Lord loves He chastens, And scourges every son whom He receives."

The next prophecy is found in John 21:18,

> 18 Most assuredly, I say to you, when you were younger, you girded yourself and walked where you wished; but when you are old, you will stretch out your hands, and another will gird you and carry you where you do not wish.

Jesus spoke this to him concerning his death. One day Peter was going to be carried away to endure a martyr's fate and all he would have had to do to free himself of this impending doom was deny Jesus.

I'm sure the scene of that night's betrayal was so etched in his mind he dared not revisit the same decision he had so foolishly made before.

Think about it. For the three days Jesus was in the grave, Peter must have been haunted in his dreams by the sound of the rooster crowing. He probably woke up in the middle of the night sweating profusely as images of his betrayal danced through his mind.

We know that Peter gathered the other disciples to go back fishing. Upon first glance, it appears that Peter was just simply diving into something recreational to try and erase the brutal images of his Messiah hanging between heaven and earth on a tree meant for thieves and murderers.

I think this was the unfolding of a much more devious plot of Satan to destroy the apostolic assignment that was given to Peter. Enticing them to go back to their previous occupation as fishermen was an easy way to reintroduce spiritual apathy back into their life. You can almost hear the devil whispering in Peter's ear, "Well, you tried, but you failed. At least you gave it a good effort. You were never really cut out for all Jesus wanted you to do. It will be easier for you to serve God doing what you do best, fishing." How many times does the enemy seek to pacify us with this same kind of lingo?

Fortunately, Jesus knew Satan's desire to "sift" Peter as wheat, and prayed in advance for him. He knew Peter would fall asleep in the Garden of Gethsemane, instead of praying, and would be an easy target for the enemy. He knew Peter would fail, but showed His sovereignty to the devil by keeping Peter in his assignment.

Sometimes our failures can actually prove to be a greater learning curve than our victories. Thomas Edison said this about failure, "I have not failed 700 times. I have not failed once. I have succeeded in proving those 700 ways will not work. When I have eliminated the ways that will not work, I will find the way that will work."[1] Peter had a second chance to find the way that would work.

---

[1] Thomas Edison on the invention of the lightbulb. quoteinvestigator.com, monthly archives July 31, 2012. Note there are several different variations of this quote. It is not certain exactly what was said.

Reunion

Then came that fateful day when Jesus arrived out on the beach searching for His twelve disillusioned disciples. John 21:1-19 records the account:

Jesus Appears to Seven Disciples

> [1] After this Jesus revealed himself again to the disciples by the Sea of Tiberias, and he revealed himself in this way. [2] Simon Peter, Thomas (called the Twin), Nathanael of Cana in Galilee, the sons of Zebedee, and two others of his disciples were together. [3] Simon Peter said to them, "I am going fishing." They said to him, "We will go with you." They went out and got into the boat, but that night they caught nothing.
>
> [4] Just as day was breaking, Jesus stood on the shore; yet the disciples did not know that it was Jesus. [5] Jesus said to them, "Children, do you have any fish?" They answered him, "No." [6] He said to them, "Cast the net on the right side of the boat, and you will find some." So they cast it, and now they were not able to haul it in, because of the quantity of fish. [7] That disciple whom Jesus loved therefore said to Peter, "It is the Lord!" When Simon Peter heard that it was the Lord, he put on his outer garment, for he was stripped for work, and threw himself into the sea. [8] The other disciples came in the boat, dragging the net full of fish, for they were not far from the land, but about a hundred yards off.
>
> [9] When they got out on land, they saw a charcoal fire in place, with fish laid out on it, and bread. [10] Jesus said to them, "Bring some of the fish that you have just caught." [11] So Simon Peter went aboard and hauled the net ashore, full of large fish, 153 of them. And although there were so many, the net was not torn. [12] Jesus said to them, "Come and have breakfast." Now none of the disciples dared ask him, "Who are you?" They knew it

was the Lord. 13 Jesus came and took the bread and gave
it to them, and so with the fish. 14 This was now the third
time that Jesus was revealed to the disciples after he was
raised from the dead.

Jesus and Peter

15 When they had finished breakfast, Jesus said to Simon
Peter, "Simon, son of John, do you love me more than
these?" He said to him, "Yes, Lord; you know that I
love you." He said to him, "Feed my lambs." 16 He said
to him a second time, "Simon, son of John, do you love
me?" He said to him, "Yes, Lord; you know that I love
you." He said to him, "Tend my sheep." 17 He said to
him the third time, "Simon, son of John, do you love
me?" Peter was grieved because he said to him the third
time, "Do you love me?" and he said to him, "Lord,
you know everything; you know that I love you." Jesus
said to him, "Feed my sheep. 18 Truly, truly, I say to
you, when you were young, you used to dress yourself and walk wherever you wanted, but when you are
old, you will stretch out your hands, and another will
dress you and carry you where you do not want to go."
19 (This he said to show by what kind of death he was
to glorify God.) And after saying this he said to him,
"Follow me" (ESV).

What an amazing reunion! Jesus came to them the second time much like He had the first. There are many striking similarities between the two. In both cases the disciples were in their boat fishing; both times they had gone a long time without catching anything; and in both scenarios Jesus gives them instruction on where the fish were located. They even bring in an amazing catch of fish just like the first time. They must have thought, "Man, the only other time we did this well fishing was the first day we met Jesus."

It is interesting to note that the disciple whom Jesus loved (John) noticed who Jesus was, not by seeing Him, but by seeing the amazing catch of fish, whereas Thomas had to touch Jesus' side and hands before he believed.

Oftentimes we think of Peter being the spiritual leader of the disciples, recognizing the hidden truths of Jesus' divinity before anyone else. We talk about him jumping out of the boat and swimming to Jesus before the rest of the disciples could get to Him.

I think the real leader of this story is John, not Peter. He recognized the ways of his Master without having to see His face. May we be the type of disciples who respond to His gentle nudgings, rather than expect to hear His booming voice!

It is amazing to think that Jesus knows exactly how to reveal Himself to us in every stage of our life. He knows that sometimes we will be too blind and calloused to recognize when He is moving, so He chooses to spark our memories by taking us back to the moment we first fell in love with Him. Only the true Romancing Redeemer and Desire of all Nations could have that kind of effect on us.

He is our portion. He does not just bless us with every spiritual blessing in the heavenly places—He *is* THE BLESSING in the heavenly places. He makes Himself available to us so that we can have all things pertaining to life and godliness. We need to let Him take us back to the moment we first gave our heart to Him.

I have been married for almost eight years. I know the quickest way to my wife's heart. All I have to do is take her back to the restaurant we dined at on the day I proposed to her. It is little reminders like these which renew affections for one another.

Jesus not only revealed where the fish were, but He also cooked all eleven disciples a meal. He served them at a time when He deserved to be served. The fish became an illustration of His love for them.

Peter had an even deeper connection to Jesus' use of fish. Not only did he see Jesus multiply the fish to feed the five thousand, but it was in the mouth of a fish he found a coin that could pay his taxes. I guarantee we would remember the day Jesus helped us pay our taxes!

With all of these instances in mind, Peter leaps from the boat, dragging this enormous catch of fish to shore. The man, who had once walked on water to get to Jesus, is now treading water to walk with Him once more. I have to believe that Peter felt Jesus would stretch out His arm once again, into the deep waters of unbelief and regret, and pull him out.

It was there on the beach where Peter locked eyes with the One who had caught a glance of him in the very act of his hypocrisy. Jesus did not come to condemn His disciples, but to commission them. Three times He spoke to Peter with these penetrating words: "Do you love Me? Feed My sheep." He was searching for Peter's heart by giving him three more chances to confess his love and allegiance to his Lord.

The man, who had once walked on water to get to Jesus, is now treading water to walk with Him once more.

The Lord is truly "slow to anger, and abounding in steadfast love." He gives us multiple chances to confess Him, even though we have denied Him so often. As Peter faced his executioners he would have had the chance to try and free himself from this punishment by denying the Lord. Instead of taking this opportunity he chose to be hung upside down on the cross. He said that he was not worthy to die right side up like his Savior.

The next time someone tries to get you to back down from your faith, recall the once cowardly Peter, who boldly stood up to his accusers, so that his final breath could be drawn in the presence of Jesus.

Chapter 2

The Infection

"People talk about the curse of sin, but they do not understand that the whole nature has been infected by sin, and that the curse is on everything. My intellect, has that been defiled by sin? Terribly, and the curse of sin is on it, and therefore my intellect must go down into the death. Ah, I believe that the Church of Christ suffers more today from trusting in intellect, in sagacity, in culture, and in mental refinement, than from almost anything else. The Spirit of the world comes in, and men seek by their wisdom, and by their knowledge, to help the Gospel, and they rob it of its crucifixion mark. Christ directed Paul to go and preach the Gospel of the cross, but to do it not with wisdom of words. The curse of sin is on all that is of nature."[2] —Andrew Murray

What if I told you there is a terrible infection that has been around longer than any other disease known to man?

[2] Andrew Murray, *The Master's Indwelling* (Chicago, New York, Toronto: Fleming H. Revell Company, 1896), 124.

Our own sin has been the cause for countless wars, genocide, homicide, abortion, human trafficking, and every other atrocity, from the fall of Adam, to the end of the age.

Not only has it been around longer than every other disease, but it is also the cause of every sickness known to man and eventually will be the cause of both your death and mine.

It is an epidemic that has infected every society, and is indifferent of age, race, and nationality. We are born into it and there is only one way out. Jesus! We are both helpless and hopeless without Him.

Our own sin has been the cause for countless wars, genocide, homicide, abortion, human trafficking, and every other atrocity, from the fall of Adam, to the end of the age; mankind will feel the sting of death. People must be told that the only way out of such plight is through the shed blood of Jesus. He is the answer to every problem we will ever face. We need Him now more than ever. The world needs Him now more than ever.

Matthew 9:35-38 (ESV) says,

> [35] And Jesus went throughout all the cities and villages,
> teaching in their synagogues and proclaiming the gospel
> of the kingdom and healing every disease and every afflic-
> tion. [36] When he saw the crowds, he had compassion for
> them, because they were harassed and helpless, like sheep
> without a shepherd. [37] Then he said to his disciples, "The
> harvest is plentiful, but the laborers are few; [38] therefore
> pray earnestly to the Lord of the harvest to send out
> laborers into his harvest."

Jesus recognized the infection. Jesus is the only physician who contains within Himself the cure for this generation. He knew the needs of His generation. Do you know the needs of this generation? Keith Green said, "This generation of believers…is responsible for this generation of souls."[3] Who is going to reach your generation? Who is going to bring them to the One who has the power to end their suffering and shame? The only plausible answer to this question is YOU! You are God's plan A. There is no plan B.

Only those who are gripped with this mission from heaven will answer its call. It is not God's job to make us answer this call. It is our job to pray until we burn with holy conviction to see lost people discover life in Jesus. Do not wander aimlessly through life insisting that God meet your every demand before you fully surrender yourself to Him. We are called to surrender all; unfortunately hell is full of people who surrendered some.

It is our job to pray until we burn with holy conviction to see lost people discover life in Jesus.

We were created for Him. Live your life with intention. Jesus urges us in Luke 9:62 to put our "hand to the plow and don't look back." Don't shrink back into your past lifestyle. Do not let your friends dictate how you will serve God. The Bible tells us to "remember Lot's wife." She wanted to have her feet in two different worlds. One world opposed the will of God, and the other called her to walk in the will of God. She wanted both. She was turned into a pillar of salt because of her double-minded attitude. This should be a warning to us.

As absurd as this may sound to you, most Christians live this way. They have not taken up their cross and followed Jesus. They keep on dropping their cross at every little amusement table the devil puts in their path. After they have their fill of one pleasure, they say to God, "I will never do that again." Then as Scripture says in Proverbs 26:11, "As a dog returns to his own vomit, so a fool repeats his folly."

---

[3] Keith Green lyrics from the song "Open Your Eyes".

We would never think of going to a major league ball game and cheer for both teams to win. We need to pick a side and commit ourselves to its cause. I choose Jesus' side, because He always wins.

This infection caused Jesus to take a proactive position. Jesus then commissioned the disciples to intercede for more workers in the field.

Intercession

Many great Christian leaders have written extensively on having a spirit of prayer. To them it was their benchmark to spiritual success. A spirit of prayer is being overwhelmingly convinced on a day-to-day basis that there is a need that requires your attention in prayer. Have you felt the need?

A spirit of prayer is being overwhelmingly convinced on a day-to-day basis that there is a need that requires your attention in prayer.

The more we seek Him, the more we understand how much people need Him. When we pray for others our connection to God helps build a link between them and His Spirit. The devil wants to destroy that link by eliminating your prayer life. It reminds me of a game I used to play in grade school called Red Rover. The idea of the game was to form a line of people all locking hands with the person next to them. There would be two lines of people, standing opposite of each other. A kid from one line would call out to a kid from the other line, "Red Rover, Red Rover, send Billy right over" (or whomever it may be that they wanted to send over) and then it was Billy's job to try and break the formation of the line by running through their interlocked hands.

The enemy is always looking for a weak spot in our union with God. He usually finds that weakness through people that we choose to lock hands with. Your relationships can make you or break you! I thank God I have a wife whom I trust and can confide in about anything. She helps hold my hand firm when I want to let go. When we are both feeling weak we know there is One whose hand is strong and can pull us up out of any pit. Hebrews 7:25 assures us that Jesus is "forever making intercession for the saints." You may ask, "How do I learn how to intercede?" We have received the greatest model of prayer and intercession from the great intercessor Himself.

The enemy is always looking for a weak spot in our union with God.

Andrew Murray said in his book, *With Christ in the School of Prayer*,

> "No one can teach like Jesus. A pupil needs a teacher who knows His work, who has the gift of teaching, who in patience and love will descend to the pupil's needs. Blessed be God! Jesus is all this and much more. It is Jesus, praying Himself, Who teaches to pray. He knows what prayer is. He learned it amid the trials and tears of His earthly life. In heaven it is still His beloved work. His life there is prayer. Nothing delights Him more than to find those whom He can take with Him into the Father's presence, clothing them with power to pray down God's blessing to those around them, training them to be His fellow-workers in the intercession by which the Kingdom is to be revealed on earth."[4]

As we draw closer to Him, we will feel His brokenness for humanity. David Brainerd, missionary to the Native Americans, would oftentimes weep uncontrollably before his hearers. This deep emotion would cause his audience to be cut to the heart with godly sorrow. His deep conviction, mixed with a profound sense of brokenness, resulted in spurring on countless missionaries

[4] Andrew Murray, *With Christ in the School of Prayer* (New Kensington, Pennsylvania: Whitaker House, 1981), 13.

and ministers such as Jonathan Edwards and John Wesley. He died at the young age of twenty-nine of tuberculosis. He left us with these penetrating words that help give us a clear picture of his position before God: "[I] could have no freedom in the thought of any other circumstances or business in life: All my desire was the conversion of the heathen, and all my hope was in God: God does not suffer me to please or comfort myself with hopes of seeing friends, returning to my dear acquaintance, and enjoying worldly comforts."[5]

To fully understand the depths of lost humanity we must allow the Holy Spirit to usher us in to the inner chambers of God's most holy place. For it is there that we understand the measureless compassion of our heavenly Father.

Get a GPS

What does it mean to be lost? In the natural to be lost means, "Unable to find one's way; not knowing one's whereabouts" (wordreference.com).[6]

What are the consequences of being lost? The fear of never being found; a stark feeling of loneliness; and never getting to see your loved ones again. None of these definitions is exhaustive or fully captures the emotions of being lost. Think of a child lost in a grocery store, desperately searching for their parents. It's terrifying for them! They have never had to care for themselves and wouldn't even know the first thing about how to take care of themselves.

What if someone is lost, but doesn't know they are lost? How many of us have been on a trip with a stubborn dad or grandpa who refuses to stop and ask for directions? In their minds they are not lost; they are just on a little scenic detour.

[5] David Brainerd, *Life and Diary of David Brainerd* (New Haven, Connecticut: The Jonathan Edwards Center at Yale University, 1749), 174.
[6] Definition from wordreference.com.

For some reason, when we get older we feel more independent and capable of taking care of ourselves. Maybe it is due to all the knowledge we acquire and as a result, our confidence continues to build. The only problem is that this can cause us to not ask for help when we need it, and that can lead to a life independent of Him.

Some people wander through life unaware of their condition before God. They don't realize that they have wronged Him in any way. To them, Jesus is just for the "church people" to be their "crutch" in life. Their hearts say, "We are strong enough to do this on our own." They are not upset with others who serve Him. They are not necessarily mad at the church. In their minds, "we are just on two different paths that will lead us to the same destination."

As believers we know that this mind-set is terribly wrong. The question is, "What are you going to do about it?" Are you content to go your own way and let them go their own way? Are you willing to let people spend an eternity in hell, just because you are unmoved by their decisions? You would never allow your child to do destructive things to himself without doing everything in your power to stop him. If you are cold and indifferent to those lost in sin, you may be under greater condemnation from the Lord than they will be.

Help Is on the "Way"

The Lord is calling you to be a minister of reconciliation. What exactly does that mean? Let's look at this Scripture in its entirety to help us clarify what God is asking us to do. Second Corinthians 5:19 says, "God was in Christ reconciling the world to Himself, not imputing their trespasses to them, and has committed to us the word of reconciliation."

To be lost from God means to be separated from His favor by our sin. Let me explain something that is very important for us to understand. God never reacts to situations because He has been somehow "caught off guard." Even in the case of original sin of Adam and Eve, God had a plan already set in place for the restitution of man to Himself. In Revelation 13:8 it says, "...the Lamb was slain from the foundation of the world."

Praise God! Jesus has cancelled our sins, and does not hold them against us. According to Galatians 3:13, "Christ has redeemed us from the curse of the law, having become a curse for us (for it is written, 'Cursed is everyone who hangs on a tree')." As believers we have the privilege of approaching the throne room of grace, but we must understand that those who have rejected the Lord will stand before Him as their judge. It is our responsibility to lead them to the mercy seat and introduce them to the One who sits enthroned on it. We must reach out to those who are lost, but first they have to realize they are lost.

We must reach out to those who are lost, but first they have to realize they are lost.

As ministers of reconciliation, we sometimes have the unenviable job of convincing unbelievers of their separation from God and the impending judgment that awaits them if they do not repent of their sins. But it is our privilege to show them that there is an advocate, Jesus, who wants to try their case before a just God. There is also an accuser, Satan, who is hell-bent on their destruction. He does not want them to be acquitted of their sins because he, himself, was not acquitted of his. He tried to exalt himself above God but was cast down from heaven along with a third of the angels.

It is our job to convince men that their best deeds, their goodness, and their charity are like "filthy rags" before God. Until they are confronted with this reality they will continue to declare their innocence.

In the case of our American judicial system, man is innocent until proven guilty. In the case of heaven's court system, man is guilty until declared innocent. John 3:18 backs this point up: “He that believeth on him is not condemned: but he that believeth not is condemned already, because he hath not believed in the name of the only begotten Son of God” (KJV). We were born guilty and only Jesus can declare us innocent. He has come “to seek and save the lost.” He would not have to seek for them if they were out in the open. Our sinful hearts cause us to try and hide things from God.

If Adam, a man whom God personally walked with did not fully understand his separation from God, what makes us think that lost people today will suddenly have an epiphany of Him?

It is just like the case with Adam and Eve. They hid themselves from God, and God asked Adam, “Where are you, Adam?” He is asking men and women the same question today. God knows where you are in relationship to His Son. He just wants you to know where you are. God knew where Adam was all the time, but Adam didn’t fully know his condition before God.

If Adam, a man whom God personally walked with did not fully understand his separation from God, what makes us think that lost people today will suddenly have an epiphany of Him?

Extreme Measures

People also need to know what extreme measures God has taken on their behalf to draw them back into fellowship with Him. Jesus gives us a glimpse into the Father heart of God through the story of the prodigal son.

Luke 15:11-32 (ESV), illustrates this story:

> 11 And he said, “There was a man who had two sons.
> 12 And the younger of them said to his father, ‘Father,
> give me the share of property that is coming to me.’

And he divided his property between them. [13] Not many days later, the younger son gathered all he had and took a journey into a far country, and there he squandered his property in reckless living. [14] And when he had spent everything, a severe famine arose in that country, and he began to be in need. [15] So he went and hired himself out to one of the citizens of that country, who sent him into his fields to feed pigs. [16] And he was longing to be fed with the pods that the pigs ate, and no one gave him anything.

[17] "But when he came to himself, he said, 'How many of my father's hired servants have more than enough bread, but I perish here with hunger! [18] I will arise and go to my father, and I will say to him, "Father, I have sinned against heaven and before you. [19] I am no longer worthy to be called your son. Treat me as one of your hired servants."' [20] And he arose and came to his father. But while he was still a long way off, his father saw him and felt compassion, and ran and embraced him and kissed him. [21] And the son said to him, 'Father, I have sinned against heaven and before you. I am no longer worthy to be called your son.' [22] But the father said to his servants, 'Bring quickly the best robe, and put it on him, and put a ring on his hand, and shoes on his feet. [23] And bring the fattened calf and kill it, and let us eat and celebrate. [24] For this my son was dead, and is alive again; he was lost, and is found.' And they began to celebrate.

[25] "Now his older son was in the field, and as he came and drew near to the house, he heard music and dancing. [26] And he called one of the servants and asked what these things meant. [27] And he said to him, 'Your brother has come, and your father has killed the fattened calf, because he has received him back safe and sound.' [28] But he was angry and refused to go in. His father came out and entreated him, [29] but he answered his father, 'Look,

> these many years I have served you, and I never disobeyed your command, yet you never gave me a young goat, that I might celebrate with my friends. [30] But when this son of yours came, who has devoured your property with prostitutes, you killed the fattened calf for him!' [31] And he said to him, 'Son, you are always with me, and all that is mine is yours. [32] It was fitting to celebrate and be glad, for this your brother was dead, and is alive; he was lost, and is found.'"

In this parable of the prodigal son, Jesus paints us a picture of a man who had everything he ever needed at his father's house. He didn't have to worry about anything. Unfortunately, the nagging thought of what he was missing out on away from his father's house lead him to make a disgraceful decision. He took an early withdrawal on his inheritance and ventured out on his own. Why, you may ask, was this disgraceful?

The Patterns of the Prodigal

First of all, his birthright should only have been collected after his father had died. It was like telling his dad, "I wish you were dead so I could have my inheritance." How many people do you know who feel God owes them something? They have an entitlement mentality. They never stop to ask, "What do I owe God?" This is how the prodigal son was acting towards his father.

Secondly, he underscored the great blessings he already had at his father's house. Every day people enjoy a life that was given them by God without even the slightest thanks or consideration towards God for their existence. The early church understood that it was "in Him that they lived, moved, and had their very existence."

Third, he wasted the inheritance his father had worked so hard to give him on riotous living. To have his hard-earned money used in such a shameful way had to bring a reproach from outsiders on this father. In the same way, imagine the suffering and shame Jesus went through on our behalf, being mocked, beaten, and hung naked on a tree for the whole world to see.

Go one step further with me and imagine the Father having to turn away from His Son because the sins of the sons of men were placed upon His shoulders. In the Hebrew culture the tabernacle veil that separated ordinary men from the Holy of Holies was considered to be the hem of God's garment. This presents us with a wonderful picture of the mourning process God went through when Jesus died. When the veil was torn from top to bottom it was as if God was rending His own garments in a heavenly lamentation. He even caused darkness to descend on the land, which ushered all creation into a place of mourning. Jesus' death represents the extreme measure God took for us. Take a moment to pause and reflect on such a great salvation that was won for us, at a tremendous cost to God. It is this thought that should challenge us to reach lost men, because that is what Jesus would do.

The Running Father

The story of the prodigal is not over; Jesus, being the masterful storyteller that He is, saved the best part of this analogy for the end. After coming to the point of losing all his money and eating pig slop, the son finally realizes his grave mistake. Many people are sitting in the same kind of stinking pigpen. They convince themselves that there is no better place for them to be. The bad thing is they eat the slop thinking it is steak. When I was younger I used to love eating frozen microwaveable dinners, but when I met my wife she introduced me to the finer foods. Now there are certain kinds of food I will no longer eat. My taste buds have evolved.

Both physically and spiritually speaking, the prodigal son's tastes changed. He reminds himself that all he's ever needed came from his father, and maybe if he goes back and humbles himself as a servant instead of a son, then his father would receive him back. As he comes over the crest of the hill his father notices him from far off and goes running to meet his son.

The more of the goodness of God we feast on, the less we desire the delicacies of sin.

He didn't welcome the boy back as a servant, but as a son. This is the way that God treats a sinner when he comes home. He kills the fattened calf and throws a big party in celebration for one who was lost but now is found. The more of the goodness of God we feast on, the less we desire the delicacies of sin.

I heard a story told by Don Wildmon that I think illustrates the prodigal and his father quite well:

> "A certain Dr. Rosenberry was riding a train, many years ago, across the state to attend a conference. There weren't many people on the train, and he noticed in his car a young man who seemed very nervous. He would take a seat, sit for a moment, get up and move. Finally Dr. Rosenberry went over to where the young man was, sat down next to him and said: 'What's your trouble, son? Is something bothering you? I'd certainly like to help, if I could.'
>
> "The young man looked at Dr. Rosenberry for a minute and then spoke up: 'I don't mind telling you. Do you know where Springvale is?' 'Yes, I think that's the next stop.' The young man spoke again: 'Yes, sir. We will be there in just a few minutes. That's my home. I lived there until three years ago. My mother and father still live there. But three years ago I had a quarrel with my father. I told him he would never see me again. I packed my bags and left. It's been hard during the past three years. Many times I've wanted to go back; I have been writing my mother. I told her I'd like to stop for a moment, that is, if it would be all right with Daddy. I told her that if Daddy said it was all right, to hang something white

outside the house where I could see it when the train passed. But I told her not to do it unless Daddy agreed. She might just do it anyway, you know.'

"There was a period of quietness, and the boy looked out the window. Then the terrain became familiar; the train was nearing the house where his parents lived. He spoke up excitedly: 'Mister, would you look for me? It's the next house, just around the bend. I just can't look. If there isn't something white…I just can't look.'

"The train slowed for the curve and jerked a bit stopping for the water tank. Nearly forgetting everything, Dr. Rosenberry just about shouted, 'Look, son, look!' The little farmhouse sat among the trees, but you could hardly see it for the white. The parents had taken everything white they could get their hands on and hung it out on the hillside. Every sheet, bedspread, towel, sock, handkerchief—everything white they could find was hung on that hillside.

"The boy became very nervous and pale. His fingers gripped the cheap suitcase. He was out of the car before it had completely stopped, and the last they saw of him he was running up the hill to his home as fast as his feet would carry him."[7]

Our heavenly Father is always waiting for the prodigal's arrival.

He has hung up everything white to remind us that as we come to Him, He has provided a way through His Son for us to be made pure. The Gospel has an amazing reciprocal value unlike any other cult or religion can offer. The Prince of Peace grants us the opportunity to be peacemakers! We have been entrusted with a divine seed to deposit in the lives of others. Even though the Gospel is over two thousand years old, it is as fresh today as it was when the first drop of blood fell from Jesus' body.

[7] Story told by Don Wildmon of The American Family Association.

Chapter 3

The Knowing

"There is not in the world a kind of life more sweet and delightful than that of a continual conversation with God."[8]
—Brother Lawrence

If we truly want to reveal God's heart to a hurting, lost, and despondent generation, we ourselves need to have daily encounters with Him. Genuine concern flows out of genuine relationship, in the same way that superficial concern flows out of superficial relationship. Nobody cares about the welfare of others quite like God. At the risk of sounding a bit redundant, allow me to clarify once again that it is because of His great love for us that He gave His Son's life as a ransom for ours.

Journey is all about discovery. Our unseen, often mysterious God has called us to go on an amazing adventure with Him. He just asks that we walk by faith, not by sight. It is sad that a lot of people do not recognize when He tries to make Himself known, or they do not recognize it until it is too late.

---

[8] Brother Lawrence, *The Practice of the Presence of God,* 5th Letter (Oxford, MS: Project Gutenberg Literary Archive Foundation, & Lightheart, 2002), 20.

Luke 24:13-35 (ESV) illustrates this point well:

On the Road to Emmaus

13 That very day two of them were going to a village named
Emmaus, about seven miles from Jerusalem, 14 and they
were talking with each other about all these things that
had happened. 15 While they were talking and discussing
together, Jesus himself drew near and went with them.
16 But their eyes were kept from recognizing him. 17 And
he said to them, "What is this conversation that you are
holding with each other as you walk?" And they stood
still, looking sad. 18 Then one of them, named Cleopas,
answered him, "Are you the only visitor to Jerusalem
who does not know the things that have happened there
in these days?" 19 And he said to them, "What things?"
And they said to him, "Concerning Jesus of Nazareth, a
man who was a prophet mighty in deed and word before
God and all the people, 20 and how our chief priests
and rulers delivered him up to be condemned to death,
and crucified him. 21 But we had hoped that he was the
one to redeem Israel. Yes, and besides all this, it is now
the third day since these things happened. 22 Moreover,
some women of our company amazed us. They were at
the tomb early in the morning, 23 and when they did
not find his body, they came back saying that they had
even seen a vision of angels, who said that he was alive.
24 Some of those who were with us went to the tomb and
found it just as the women had said, but him they did
not see." 25 And he said to them, "O foolish ones, and
slow of heart to believe all that the prophets have spoken!
26 Was it not necessary that the Christ should suffer these
things and enter into his glory?" 27 And beginning with
Moses and all the Prophets, he interpreted to them in all
the Scriptures the things concerning himself.

> 28 So they drew near to the village to which they were going. He acted as if he were going farther, 29 but they urged him strongly, saying, "Stay with us, for it is toward evening and the day is now far spent." So he went in to stay with them. 30 When he was at table with them, he took the bread and blessed and broke it and gave it to them. 31 And their eyes were opened, and they recognized him. And he vanished from their sight. 32 They said to each other, "Did not our hearts burn within us while he talked to us on the road, while he opened to us the Scriptures?" 33 And they rose that same hour and returned to Jerusalem. And they found the eleven and those who were with them gathered together, 34 saying, "The Lord has risen indeed, and has appeared to Simon!" 35 Then they told what had happened on the road, and how he was known to them in the breaking of the bread.

I have heard Christians fantasize about what it would be like to live during the time Jesus walked on the earth. I guess it is always easier to view life from the past or the future, instead of the present.

Have you ever thought, "If I lived in ancient Israel at that time, I would have recognized who Jesus claimed to be"? Would we have been as unaware of Him as the disciples were on the road to Emmaus?

They walked with Jesus without even realizing His true identity. It even says in verse 27 that He expounded to them out of the Scriptures who He was. How many of us have become so dull to the reality of His presence we do not even realize when He is walking right beside us? His desire is to make Himself known so that our hearts will burn with a fresh understanding of how truly close He is.

His desire is to make Himself known so that our hearts will burn with a fresh understanding of how truly close He is.

When Jesus illuminates our hearts to the reality of His presence the results are unmistakable and dramatic. These disciples cannot keep their experience with the Lord to themselves, so they run and tell the other disciples what happened. As our hearts are awakened to the reality of His presence in our life, I guarantee we will have to tell someone about our encounter.

Jesus performed miracles for countless people and then instructed them to remain silent. The outcome always seemed the same. As soon as Jesus left they would broadcast their miracle to whomever would listen.

My mom always told me that I was terrible at keeping secrets. When I was younger I remember going to her and saying, "Mom, I know I should not tell you this, but…." Then what was supposed to remain a secret spewed out of my mouth. I would have been an awful spy, but a great informant.

We need to be careful about broadcasting what was meant to stay between us and the Lord. The good news is that it is never wrong to proclaim the Good News. If you have an itch to share unknown information, start by being a "steward of the mysteries of Christ."

"Awaken Our Hearts, Lord!"

I remember being in a powerful church service several years ago where the kids in our church were so moved by the Holy Spirit they began to lay hands on and pray for the adults who were in attendance. It was one of the most genuine visitations of His presence that I have ever seen.

After service was over, I went to a local hamburger spot to grab a bite to eat. Upon entering, a friend of my brother's walked up and began talking to me. I could immediately smell the stench of alcohol emanating from his breath. I spoke with him about what had happened in that night's service. He listened intently. I could tell the Lord was drawing his heart to a place of repentance. The next day this same guy came to my house, but this time he was sober. He was ready to begin taking the first steps to becoming a disciple of Christ.

I befriended him and started pouring into him what I knew. It wasn't much, but I began to see a dramatic transformation. He would come to me often and tell me about witnessing to people and leading them to Christ. We would go to the store and he would want to talk to people about Jesus. At times I would be convicted from seeing his passion. May we all have that "first love" experience kindled in our hearts for the Lord!

In John chapter 4, Jesus goes to get a drink of water at Jacob's well. A woman from Samaria was there drawing water. In verses 9-15 Jesus asks her for a drink:

> [9] The Samaritan woman said to him, "How is it that you, a Jew, ask for a drink from me, a woman of Samaria?" (For Jews have no dealings with Samaritans.) [10] Jesus answered her, "If you knew the gift of God, and who it is that is saying to you, 'Give me a drink,' you would have asked him, and he would have given you living water."
> [11] The woman said to him, "Sir, you have nothing to draw water with, and the well is deep. Where do you get that living water? [12] Are you greater than our father Jacob? He gave us the well and drank from it himself, as did his sons and his livestock." [13] Jesus said to her, "Everyone who drinks of this water will be thirsty again,
> [14] but whoever drinks of the water that I will give him will never be thirsty again. The water that I will give him will become in him a spring of water welling up to eternal life." [15] The woman said to him, "Sir, give me this water, so that I will not be thirsty or have to come here to draw water."" (ESV).

Who would have ever thought a conversation about well water would have resulted in a whole village coming to believe

We need to take advantage of the seemingly unimportant meetings, because these may be the very ones through which God displays His mighty power.

on Jesus! This is exactly how the story ends. We need to take advantage of the seemingly unimportant meetings, because these may be the very ones through which God displays His mighty power.

Sometimes all it takes is asking the right questions so you can get the right response. Jesus knew how to spark her intrigue. He knew what questions would peak her interest. As Jesus peeled off the layers of her life, she opened up to Him like a flower does to the rays of sunlight in spring.

It's not always about asking *any* question; it's about asking the *right* questions. And it's not always about being around *any* person; it's about being around the *right* person. There is a right person to give you the right answer at the exact time you need it. That right person is God.

James says, "If any of you lacks wisdom, let him ask of God, who gives to all liberally and without reproach, and it will be given to him" (James 1:5). He also says that, "Every good gift and every perfect gift is from above, and comes down from the Father of lights, with whom there is no variation or shadow of turning" (James 1:17).

God wants you to have thorough knowledge of Him and His ways. If you do not believe that, let me share a few Scriptures with you:

> Psalm 46:10: "Be still, and know that I am God: I will be exalted among the nations, I will be exalted in the earth!"
>
> Jeremiah 24:7: "Then I will give them a heart to know Me, that I am the Lord; and they shall be My people, and I will be their God, for they shall return to Me with their whole heart."

John 10:27: "My sheep hear My voice, and I know them, and they follow Me:"

Ephesians 1:17-19 says,

> [17] that the God of our Lord Jesus Christ, the Father of glory, may give to you the spirit of wisdom and revelation in the knowledge of Him, [18] the eyes of your understanding being enlightened; that you may know what is the hope of His calling, what are the riches of the glory of His inheritance in the saints, [19] and what is the exceeding greatness of His power toward us who believe, according to the working of His mighty power.

Building History with God

Charles Spurgeon in his devotional *Morning and Evening*, pg. 244:

> You call me to Yourself by saying, "Come away," and this is a melodious call indeed. To come to You is to come home from exile, to come to land out of the raging storm, to come to rest after long labor, to come to the goal of my desires and the summit of my wishes. But Lord how can a stone rise, or how can a lump of clay come away from the horrible pit? Oh, raise me; draw me. Your grace can do it. Send forth Your Holy Spirit to kindle sacred flames of love in my heart, and I will continue to rise until I leave life and time behind me, and indeed "come away."[9]

Do you remember a room in your house that was off-limits to you? Maybe it was your mother and father's room. Maybe it was the room your mom kept her fine china, or a room where your dad kept valuable sports memorabilia. You were told never to play there or you would suffer the consequences.

---

[9] Charles Spurgeon, *Morning and Evening* (Radford, VA: Wilder Publications, 2009), 244.

As sons and daughters of God there are no rooms off-limits to His children. He trusts us enough to give us unlimited access to His heavenly places. God wants us to enjoy His presence so much that He allows us to go into His most secret place. It's in this secret place where we build our own personal history with God.

For every Christian, building their own history with God is a must! The Bible is not just a list of do's and don'ts. It is a book full of the personal stories of ordinary men and women. The only thing special about these people was their disposition before God. David was a man after God's own heart, even though he committed adultery and then murdered a man to cover up this terrible sin. It is stories like this that give us hope, especially when we see the broken pieces of our life put back together by God's unseen hand.

Of course the Bible is also full of the stories of people who left rotten legacies. When God offered these people a second chance, they tried to take advantage of Him instead of taking advantage of their newfound opportunity. Saul is one of these people.

1 Samuel 19:9-24 (ESV):

> [9] Then a harmful spirit from the Lord came upon Saul, as
> he sat in his house with his spear in his hand. And David
> was playing the lyre. [10] And Saul sought to pin David
> to the wall with the spear, but he eluded Saul, so that
> he struck the spear into the wall. And David fled and
> escaped that night.
>
> [11] Saul sent messengers to David's house to watch him,
> that he might kill him in the morning. But Michal,
> David's wife, told him, "If you do not escape with your
> life tonight, tomorrow you will be killed." [12] So Michal
> let David down through the window, and he fled away
> and escaped. [13] Michal took an image and laid it on the
> bed and put a pillow of goats' hair at its head and covered
> it with the clothes. [14] And when Saul sent messengers to
> take David, she said, "He is sick." [15] Then Saul sent the

messengers to see David, saying, "Bring him up to me in
the bed, that I may kill him." 16 And when the messengers came in, behold, the image was in the bed, with the
pillow of goats' hair at its head. 17 Saul said to Michal,
"Why have you deceived me thus and let my enemy go,
so that he has escaped?" And Michal answered Saul, "He
said to me, 'Let me go. Why should I kill you?'"

18 Now David fled and escaped, and he came to Samuel
at Ramah and told him all that Saul had done to him.
And he and Samuel went and lived at Naioth. 19 And it
was told Saul, "Behold, David is at Naioth in Ramah."
20 Then Saul sent messengers to take David, and when
they saw the company of the prophets prophesying, and
Samuel standing as head over them, the Spirit of God
came upon the messengers of Saul, and they also prophesied. 21 When it was told Saul, he sent other messengers, and they also prophesied. And Saul sent messengers
again the third time, and they also prophesied. 22 Then
he himself went to Ramah and came to the great well
that is in Secu. And he asked, "Where are Samuel and
David?" And one said, "Behold, they are at Naioth in
Ramah." 23 And he went there to Naioth in Ramah. And
the Spirit of God came upon him also, and as he went he
prophesied until he came to Naioth in Ramah. 24 And he
too stripped off his clothes, and he too prophesied before
Samuel and lay naked all that day and all that night.
Thus it is said, "Is Saul also among the prophets?"

Behind Closed Doors

I think this story helps give us a great contrast between King Saul's private devotion life and his public reign as king. There was a certain image that he strived to maintain in public, but was not able to, because his private relationship with God was in shambles. In verse 9 we see that God actually causes a tormenting spirit to come upon Saul.

I believe that Saul had already aligned himself with this spirit and God was giving him over to what he had already come into agreement with. Paul told Timothy to expel a man in the Corinthian church who was sleeping with his own mother-in-law. He instructed Timothy to turn this man over to the devil. Jesus said that "we can't serve two masters, because we will end up loving one and hating the other." Whichever one we spend the most time with is the one we will love.

The contrast in Saul's life comes when he meets up with the school of prophets and he begins to prophesy. He acts one way behind closed doors and another way out in the open. He was around the company of the prophets long enough to have the Spirit of God that was on them come upon him. He was having this experience vicariously through the prophets.

Anyone can prophesy when they are in the company of the prophets. Anyone can pray when they are in the company of the intercessors. Anyone can worship when they are in the company of worshippers. True depth of Christianity is not found camping out by other people's accomplishments; rather it is found by approaching the throne room of grace yourself, and receiving from God help and grace in your time of need.

It makes me wonder how many well-meaning Christians have ever gone to a special meeting with the intention of having some man or woman of God pray for them so that they would receive a greater anointing. We probably all have at some point or another.

I do believe there are times when we receive a special grace from God through their prayers, but do we ever stop and consider what that person had to go through to get to that place?

Elisha received a double portion of Elijah's ministry only after he served Elijah. Then after he received that double portion he still had to obey God's leading.

How hungry are you for God? How hungry are you for the gifts of God? Are you willing to go through what seems like hell on earth so you can experience heaven on earth?

Let's never use private intimacy with God as a means to get something publicly from Him.

As with Saul, God may cause a special anointing to come to rest on us for a time, but it is up to us to continue to invest ourselves into God and His plan for our lives in order to maintain that blessing. Let's never use private intimacy with God as a means to get something publicly from Him. Marriages fail all of the time because either the husband or the wife treats each other like this. They withhold intimacy, or give intimacy as a way of coercing their significant other to do what they want. This is manipulation, and is not much different than the actions of a prostitute. So if it is wrong in the natural, it's wrong in the spiritual.

Personal intimacy with God should always come before public display. If our ministry does not flow out of fellowship with God, it will fail. If our friendships do not flow out of communion with God, they will be shallow. If our marriages do not flow out of partnership with God, they will fall apart. If our home life does not flow out of relationship with God, it will crumble. Everything we do must be rooted and grounded in Him. Jesus is our "chief cornerstone."

The Chief Cornerstone

Without the chief cornerstone the whole building falls apart. It is the platform on which the majority of the weight of the structure rests on. If He is not our foundation our whole house is similar to a house of cards. No matter how well you build a house of cards they are still just cards. A good stiff breeze will always blow them over.

To check the quality of the foundation of a house, a qualified inspector is needed to run over all the nooks and crannies of the house with a fine-tooth comb. He is able to see damage that is hidden from the naked eye. God sees the damage in our structures that we cannot see. He is the unseen anchor of our soul. In Him we live, we move, and we have our very existence. He is literally the glue that holds us together.

He has sent His Holy Spirit to be our *parakletos,* an intercessor, consoler, advocate, comforter. The book of Joel talks about parasites that eat up the land called locusts. He then prophesies of the Spirit coming to restore the "years the swarming locusts have eaten."

Some of our houses are eaten up by termites. The outside of the home appears beautiful, but the bones of the home are eaten away. The more we allow Jesus into the walls of our heart, the more exterminating He will do. He will bring the secret sins to the light. We all know what happens when you shine the light on the creepy crawlies; they scatter. As we draw closer to Him through His Word we will have a "lamp to our feet and a light to our path." Proverbs 20:27 says, "The spirit of a man is the lamp of the Lord, searching all the inner depths of his heart." We were not designed to function outside of relationship with God.

Why did God make us that way? To create in us utter dependence upon Him and His Spirit. We put our hope and trust in Him, because He is able and willing to meet every need we may face. Until we come to this point we will continue to hit our head up against a seemingly impenetrable wall.

David says in Psalm 18:29, "For by You I can run against a troop, by my God I can leap over a wall." David was a man who understood how to lean on the strong arm of the Lord. Charles Spurgeon said, "The right kind of independency is the independency of the man who knows no dependence except upon God."[10] Do not continue to run into a wall you were meant to

[10] Charles Spurgeon in his sermon "Waiting only upon God". Delivered on Sabbath Morning, August 2, 1857, at the Music Hall, Royal Surrey Gardens.

leap over. That is the very definition of insanity. God wants us to trust that He has the power to change any situation; that He can make the impossible, possible. It is time for us to speak to our mountains by faith. God is waiting for us to declare with boldness His purpose, so that His will may be done on earth as it is in heaven.

It is who you are in the secret place with God that will define you!

Psalm 91:1-2 says, "He who dwells in the secret place of the most High will abide under the shadow of the Almighty. I will say of the Lord, 'He is my refuge and my fortress: my God; in him will I trust.'" It is who you are in the secret place with God that will define you!

Chapter 4

Colliding Cultures

Whether you realize it or not, we are all on a journey with God. We are either following Him or running from Him. The Bible calls Him our forerunner. A forerunner is someone who goes ahead of the rest of the pack, preparing a way for them. He takes on the challenge of clearing out all of the underbrush so others can walk through what he had to work through.

Have you ever heard the term trailblazer? I grew up in a small town in Illinois. I have been down my fair share of trails. Some of them were well worn and easy to follow, but others were grown over with thick foliage. It is always difficult to navigate through dense forest. Most of the well-worn trails were made that way over time by hunters with four-wheelers.

When you are following Jesus there is no trail that you will go down that He hasn't already made a path for you.

When you are following Jesus there is no trail that you will go down that He hasn't already made a path for you.

If He is our forerunner, then that means He is setting the pace. Galatians 5:25 says, "If we live in the Spirit, let us also walk in the Spirit."

One version says to keep in step with the Spirit. We serve a God who never sleeps or slumbers. God is not in the habit of slowing down, so if we plan on following Him we need to keep pace. When we are not following Him, then we are naturally distancing ourselves from Him.

There is no obligation on God's part to come follow us when we have turned from Him. In Hebrews it says, "His soul takes no pleasure in those who shrink back."

Colossians 3:2 says, "Set your affection on things above, not on things on the earth" (KJV). It matters where and on whom we direct our affection. God desires to be the center of our affection. Not only does He desire it, He commands it.

In our culture we tend to view Christianity through rose-tinted glasses. It is kind of like looking through a kaleidoscope. We see the parts we want to see, the things that feel the best to us, and the things that require the least out of us.

Your beliefs and values will inevitably be dictated by whatever culture you choose to yield to the most.

As humans we have a tendency, whether consciously or subconsciously, to make up an image of God in our minds that best suits our current needs. This is called humanism. We were made in His image, but oftentimes we try to make God in our image. That is called idol worship.

Whether we realize it or not, the culture that we grew up in and live in plays a huge part in our own moral climate. This by no means gives us an excuse to live life however feels best to us.

The truth is your beliefs and values will inevitably be dictated by whatever culture you choose to yield to the most. We've been told that conformity is wrong, but my question is, "Is there a culture that is okay to conform to?" The answer is ABSOLUTELY! It should be our life's mission to impress upon this earth the realities of heaven.

> **If the culture is always changing, what will define you?**

God wanted to be with us so much on this journey that He sent His Holy Spirit to live in us. He knows that we cannot walk this journey alone. We are completely dependent upon Him. Many times God will take us through places in our life that seem uncomfortable so we will learn to trust Him to do the impossible.

We have His culture living in us, while at the same time walking in another culture. Not only are there two cultures, but the two cultures are complete opposites.

Let's take a closer look at these two different cultures or kingdoms. One is a Kingdom that never changes because it has never had to change; the other is a kingdom that is always in transition, and the foundation is constantly unstable.

If you look through a kaleidoscope you will notice a vast array of swirling colors and the only consistent thing about its image is its inconsistency. The culture of this world is like that. Instead of having set values that dictate the way we live, whatever is the most current, in-style fad available is what people flock to.

Nobody wants a flip phone; they want a smart phone. Nobody wants a regular iPad; they want the latest version of the iPad. And if you are "trending" on Twitter, then it looks like you made it to your fifteen minutes of fame.

Tell me, in ten years, what will be the next big thing? Nobody can answer that. So if the culture is always changing, what will define you?

Mirror, Mirror, on the Wall

When you look in the mirror, what does it tell you? A mirror shows us some things we want to see, and a lot we don't want to see. Some would say, "Image isn't important," but to God, image is very important. He thought so much about humanity that we were the only species created in His image. When it came to creating us, God saved His best creation for the final day.

God has a mirror and it does not lie. The culture also has a mirror and it is very deceitful. Which mirror will you believe? Truth be told, we care a lot more about our image than what we let on.

Think of all the magazines that center around this unrealistic image of beauty. If you are married, or have daughters living with you, you probably have these magazines randomly strung around the house. They have become so popular because they feed off our self-conscious emotions, fueling our imaginations with vain thoughts of what "we are supposed to look like."

Christ paid much too high a price for us not to accept who He made us to be.

We must always understand that God's view of image and beauty is different from the world. The culture will lie to you and tell you how you should dress, or what your body should look like. The devil wants to destroy the image you have of yourself and of God.

Feelings of insignificance are probably one of the worst epidemics of the modern church, for both women and men. If I feel insignificant and worthless it will immobilize me.

Christ paid much too high a price for us not to accept who He made us to be. When we try to mirror the reality of someone else, we short-change God's calling on our life. The devil's scheme from the very beginning was to distort the identity of the image bearers.

Image Bearers

When Adam became conscience of his sin, he lost his sense of sonship toward his heavenly Father. This led to disillusionment about his identity for 235 years until his grandson Enosh was born. Genesis 4:26 says, "And as for Seth, to him also a son was born; and he called his name Enosh: then men began to call on the name of the Lord." This phrase can more accurately be translated, "...then men began to call themselves by the name of the Lord."

We do not merely work for God; that would make us employees. We work with God; that makes us associates, and even more than that, it makes us sons. C. S. Lewis said, "The Son of God became a man to enable men to become sons of God."[11]

Romans 8:14-19, tells us about God's plan of adopting us as sons. All creation is waiting in earnest expectation for us to walk in our God-given sonship. My sonship honors God best whenever I look the most like Him. The greatest statement that can be said of us in association with God is that "the apple doesn't fall far from the tree."

Mirroring the culture to reach the culture is called relevance. Mirroring Jesus to reach the culture is called Kingdom.

We are not seeking to be the most relevant, but the most Kingdom-minded.

Relevance without the Kingdom is just a club. The VFW is relevant; the nightclub is relevant; and to some, abortion is relevant. We are not seeking to be the most relevant, but the most Kingdom-minded. First Corinthians 15:49 says, "And as we have borne the image of the earthy, we shall also bear the image of the heavenly" (KJV). As sons of God, we are called to mirror and manifest the hidden realities of His Kingdom.

God wants to change the perceptions we have of ourselves. Second Corinthians 5:17 says, "Therefore, if anyone is in Christ,

[11] C. S. Lewis, *Mere Christianity* (San Francisco: Harper San Francisco; Revised & Enlarged Edition, 2009), 178.

he is a new creation; old things have passed away; behold, all things have become new." Second Corinthians 3:18 says, "But we all, with unveiled face, beholding as in a mirror the glory of the Lord, are being transformed into the same image from glory to glory, just as by the Spirit of the Lord."

Romans 12:1-2 says,

> [1] I beseech you therefore, brethren, by the mercies of God, that you present your bodies a living sacrifice, holy, acceptable to God, which is your reasonable service. [2] And do not be conformed to this world, but be transformed by the renewing of your mind, that you may prove what is that good and acceptable and perfect will of God.

This Scripture tells me two things:

1. Whichever culture we choose to conform to the longest will eventually transform us.
2. Without a transformed mind I will not be able to distinguish what God's will is for my life.

Even though we live in this world, we must not live our lives according to the pattern of this world. That may sound old-fashioned and religious to you, but it is the truth. His call to us is to surrender all.

It's Time

Ecclesiastes 3:1-8:

To everything *there is* a season,
A time for every purpose under heaven:
[2] A time to be born,
    And a time to die;
A time to plant,
    And a time to pluck *what is* planted;
[3] A time to kill,
    And a time to heal;

A time to break down,
And a time to build up;
4 A time to weep,
And a time to laugh;
A time to mourn,
And a time to dance;
5 A time to cast away stones,
And a time to gather stones;
A time to embrace,
And a time to refrain from embracing;
6 A time to gain,
And a time to lose;
A time to keep,
And a time to throw away;
7 A time to tear,
And a time to sew;
A time to keep silence,
And a time to speak;
8 A time to love,
And a time to hate;
A time of war,
And a time of peace.

What are you waiting for? It's time to become proactive about the things of God. Don't you think we have wasted enough of our lives consumed with ourselves? Our schedules have crowded anything to do with God out of our lives. It's time to be fired up about Jesus! It's time for us to live our lives for Him like there is no tomorrow! It's time for another Great Awakening! Remember, the Holy Spirit lives in you—not the wimpy spirit, not the cowardly spirit, and not the backslidden spirit!

Remember, the Holy Spirit lives in you—not the wimpy spirit, not the cowardly spirit, and not the backslidden spirit!

If you are looking at your life through a kaleidoscope, it's time to start looking through another lens. God's lens isn't fuzzy, it isn't confusing, and it is never out of focus. If your life is out of focus it is because you have been looking through the wrong lens.

It is time to turn your eyes upon Jesus and look full into His beautiful face, and the things of earth will grow strangely dim in the light of His glory and grace (Helen H. Lemmel, 1922).[12]

The Tale of Two Valleys

The Road Not Taken

Two roads diverged in a yellow wood,
And sorry I could not travel both
And be one traveler, long I stood
And looked down one as far as I could
To where it bent in the undergrowth;
Then took the other, as just as fair,
And having perhaps the better claim
Because it was grassy and wanted wear,
Though as for that the passing there
Had worn them really about the same,
And both that morning equally lay
In leaves no step had trodden black.
Oh, I marked the first for another day!
Yet knowing how way leads on to way
I doubted if I should ever come back.
I shall be telling this with a sigh
Somewhere ages and ages hence:
Two roads diverged in a wood, and I,
I took the one less traveled by,
And that has made all the difference.[13]

—Robert Frost

[12] Helen H. Lemmel, hymn, 1922.
[13] Robert Frost, poem, "The Road Not Taken".

As is so eloquently spoken by Robert Frost, there lies before each person two roads: one road that is the easy road, and the other that is the least travelled by men. We have a tendency to choose the "path of least resistance." Jesus talked about this very thing when He said there is a "broad road that leads to destruction and there are many who find it, but there is a narrow road that leads to life and few be who find it" (Matthew 7:13-14).

As human beings our minds are trapped in an ongoing tug-of-war. As Paul says in Romans 8:6, "The carnal mind is death, but the mind of the spirit is life and peace." God created us with the ability to choose. We choose to love Him, or we choose to hate Him. There is no in-between ground. Those who are neutral are really against God, but those are the very ones who we are told to reach.

Those who are neutral are really against God, but those are the very ones who we are told to reach.

The Bible gives us an example of two different valleys in Psalm 23 and Ezekiel 37. Both are valleys that are surrounded by death. One is just a shadow of death and the other is the very presence of death. Even though there are striking similarities between the two, there is a world of difference.

Psalm 23:4 says, "Yea, though I walk through the valley of the shadow of death, I will fear no evil; For You are with me; Your rod and Your staff, they comfort me."

In Psalm 23, David takes courage in the fact that this ominous valley was not to be feared because the Lord was with him. David is described as "a man after God's own heart." Over and over in the book of Psalms we glimpse an image of him crying out to God. We understand that David longs for the Lord; that God has captured his heart. He was the one who penned the words in Psalm 27:4: "One thing have I desired of the Lord, that will I seek after; that I may dwell in the house of the Lord all the days of my life, to behold the beauty of the Lord, and to enquire in his temple."

From an early age David's heart was filled with worship and awe of his Creator. He played his harp skillfully before the Lord as he tended his father's sheep. God took notice of his devotion. He called David and anointed him through Samuel the prophet.

God's Spirit has enabled His sons and daughters to enjoy unending communion with Jesus. He has set our hearts free from the corruption of sin. Now we can boldly and confidently walk through the messes of life with the gentle assurance of God's overshadowing presence. David walked through the shadow of death while being overshadowed by the giver of Life. David's comfort came from the Comforter.

As believers, our valleys are only shadows of death. We have inherited eternal life. When we die we will shed our external shell of a body and take on a glorified body. Paul said of himself that absence from his body meant that he was present with the Lord.

Hebrews 9:27 says, "And as it is appointed unto men once to die, but after this the judgment" (KJV). One out of every one people dies. This is a fact of this earthly life. Our decision about eternity will determine our destination. As believers, we will stand before the judgment seat of Christ and receive our rewards. Not everyone has this hope.

Death Valley

Some people are trapped in a different kind of valley. In Ezekiel 37 we see a picture of a valley of death. It is not just the shadow of death; it is a literal graveyard. Many people live there. They don't understand their condition before God. They don't know they have sinned against Him. They don't see that they are separated and alienated from Him. They don't understand that Jesus is their only hope of salvation. They are the blind leading the blind, giving false assurance to each other. They have a veil over their eyes. They need a wake-up call! We need a wake-up call!

Listen to the words of Ezekiel as he describes this valley:

> 1 The hand of the Lord was upon me, and he brought
> me out in the Spirit of the Lord and set me down in the
> middle of the valley; it was full of bones. 2 And he led me
> around among them, and behold, there were very many
> on the surface of the valley, and behold, they were very
> dry. 3 And he said to me, "Son of man, can these bones
> live?" And I answered, "O Lord God, you know." 4 Then
> he said to me, "Prophesy over these bones, and say to
> them, O dry bones, hear the word of the Lord. 5 Thus
> says the Lord God to these bones: Behold, I will cause
> breath to enter you, and you shall live. 6 And I will lay
> sinews upon you, and will cause flesh to come upon you,
> and cover you with skin, and put breath in you, and you
> shall live, and you shall know that I am the Lord."
>
> 7 So I prophesied as I was commanded. And as I proph-
> esied, there was a sound, and behold, a rattling, and the
> bones came together, bone to its bone. 8 And I looked,
> and behold, there were sinews on them, and flesh had
> come upon them, and skin had covered them. But there
> was no breath in them. 9 Then he said to me, "Prophesy
> to the breath; prophesy, son of man, and say to the
> breath, Thus says the Lord God: Come from the four
> winds, O breath, and breathe on these slain, that they
> may live." 10 So I prophesied as he commanded me, and
> the breath came into them, and they lived and stood on
> their feet, an exceedingly great army.
>
> 11 Then he said to me, "Son of man, these bones are the
> whole house of Israel. Behold, they say, 'Our bones are
> dried up, and our hope is lost; we are indeed cut off.'
> 12 Therefore prophesy, and say to them, Thus says the
> Lord God: Behold, I will open your graves and raise

> you from your graves, O my people. And I will bring you into the land of Israel. [13] And you shall know that I am the Lord, when I open your graves, and raise you from your graves, O my people. [14] And I will put my Spirit within you, and you shall live, and I will place you in your own land. Then you shall know that I am the Lord; I have spoken, and I will do it, declares the Lord." (Ezekiel 37:1-14, ESV).

Ezekiel just got dropped into the biggest reality check of his life. His mission became much more evident the day God gave him the vision of the dry bones. Sometimes we do things for God because that's what we are supposed to do.

God wants you to get a real picture of what is taking place in your generation, even if it means putting you in an uncomfortable situation you never planned for.

When was the last time you did something for God because you were gripped by what you had seen? God caused Ezekiel to see a very real picture of the house of Israel. Notice, Ezekiel never asked to be dropped into a boneyard. God wants you to get a real picture of what is taking place in your generation, even if it means putting you in an uncomfortable situation you never planned for.

We must take an honest look at two things:

1. **Our condition before God:** If our hearts are distant from Him we have no right to compel other people to come to Him. It doesn't take someone very long to see where you stand with God. I've found that an unbeliever has no problem putting you in your place if you are preaching a message that is opposite of your lifestyle. The last thing we want to do is dishonor the name of Jesus by being hypocrites. When we think of taking the Lord's name in vain we automatically think of it being used as a curse word. We also take His name in vain by living a

contradictory lifestyle to the one we confess to live. Jesus said, "Woe to him by whom offenses come" (Luke 17:1). We need to "remove the plank from our own eye, before we can see clearly to remove the speck from someone else's eye" (Matthew 7:5). Get your own heart right with God before trying to get someone else's heart right with Him! Ezekiel's heart was right with God, and that's why God made him a spokesman to the house of Israel.

2. **Others' condition before God:** May we never become so satisfied with our own salvation that we forget about reaching others with His saving grace. God asks Ezekiel in verse 3, "Son of man can these bones live?" So Ezekiel answered, "O, Lord God, You know." God does not expect you to know everything. He wants you to trust Him for the right answer. God always has the right answer for humanity. We are told in the book of Revelation that "the Lamb was slain before the foundation of the world." In His sovereignty He knew man would sin; that's why He made a way before one was ever even needed.

The wonderful thing about these two valleys is that God is actively involved in both: nurturing and restoring our broken relationship with Him. Even in the midst of his valley David knew God was with him. Ezekiel was taken by the Spirit of the Lord to the Valley of Dry Bones. It should be a comforting thought to us that God already knows where our valleys will be and He has devised a future plan of escape.

God wants to turn your valley of the shadow of death (i.e. your job, school, neighborhood, etc.) into a thriving community of believers.

In Ezekiel 37, God prepared Ezekiel to prophesy life to those who were dead. God wants to turn your valley of the shadow of death (i.e. your job, school, neighborhood, etc.) into a thriving community of believers. It's time for you to answer His call to action.

I am reminded of a story I read about the Azusa Street Revival. A group of teenage girls who attended the revival were so burdened for souls that they led a door-to-door witnessing campaign, in which over one hundred people received salvation.[14]

God's solution to resurrect a whole graveyard is found in Ezekiel 37:4: "Again He said to me, 'Prophesy to these bones and say to them, "O dry bones, hear the word of the Lord!"'" God has called us to speak to those dead in their trespasses and sins. He tells us to speak the Word of the Lord to them. If we open wide our mouths He will fill it with good things. It is time for us to use our words to bring life to people, not death.

The Wellspring of Life

In high school I played football from my sophomore to senior year. I remember the beginning of the season being the toughest. Not only was it the hottest time of the year, but we also had to practice twice a day. At times it seemed as if the sun was melting me like some kind of wax figure exposed to too much heat. It was in those moments that I truly understood what it meant to be parched. When coach would let us get a drink, we resembled a heard of animals on the Serengeti, forcibly staking our claim next to the watering hole.

I wonder what it would take for us to get so spiritually thirsty for Him that we would unashamedly position ourselves before Jesus, the Fountain of Life. The good thing is that His river never runs dry. In Psalm 42:1 David compares his thirst to a "deer panting for the water brooks." Jesus is our wellspring of life. If you are thirsty, don't go to the rancid, polluted streams of the world for refreshing—go to the One who is described as the "Fountain of Life." If we drink of Him we will never thirst again, but He will be in us "like a well springing up into everlasting life."

[14] Larry Keefauver, M.Div., *The Original Azusa Street Devotional* (Lake Mary, FL: Creation House, 1997).

Our thirst for more of Him causes other people to want Him. It is amazing to me how easy it is for us to become so dehydrated without even recognizing it. The world does not know it needs Him. They do not know their own souls are dry and empty apart from Him. We are called the salt of the earth, partly because salt causes thirst. Salt that has lost its ability to create thirst is good for nothing.

We are called the salt of the earth, partly because salt causes thirst.

Psalm 84:6-7: "When they reach Dry Valley, springs start flowing, and the Autumn rain fills it with pools of water. Your people grow stronger, and You, the God of gods, will be seen in Zion." If you've been in the valley so long that you've named your valley, it's probably time to move on. We need to start speaking to the springs in our valley to open up while we're still in our valley.

Most of society is in a valley. Ezekiel was taken to a valley to prophesy life to a graveyard, so don't be surprised if you ask for souls and God gives you a spiritual cemetery. You might be the only life those rickety bones have seen. Faith compels you to speak to your graveyards and make them God's springs. Wherever we go, springs should start flowing.

Your faith has the ability to bring refreshing to the weary. Isaiah 50:4 says, "The Lord God hath given me the tongue of the learned, that I should know how to speak a word in season to him that is weary: He wakeneth morning by morning, He wakeneth mine ear to hear as the learned" (KJV). Lord, awaken a generation to hear as the learned!

We have the responsibility and privilege of communicating the greatest message, about the greatest King, in the greatest time of need this world has ever seen.

Chapter 5

The Indispensable Ingredient

Hebrews 11:6: "But without faith it is impossible to please Him, for he who comes to God must believe that He is, and that He is a rewarder of those who diligently seek Him."

Whether we realize it or not, our culture has been conditioning us to think that our greatest level of success can only be attained when we reach our independence. How many of you have ever been told by your teachers and even your parents, "One day you are going to be out on your own and then you will have to learn how to stand on your own two feet"? What a bunch of nonsense! We all have a network of people we rely on. If you have a job you rely on your employer to pay you. If you do not have a job you rely on the government. When you are sick you rely on the doctor. When you are hungry you rely on the farmer and the grocery store. There is never a day that goes by that we are not depending on someone. This is how God intended it to be.

The self-reliance message infiltrating our culture is actually a God-defiance message. Its teaching has its roots in the New Age Movement, which believes that we are our own "god" and we need no one else to help us along on our journey. The Bible emphatically opposes this kind of heresy! This is a doctrine of devils that is damning the souls of men and women to hell! It has the appearance of godliness, but denies the power thereof.

John Calvin describes it this way:

> Mingled vanity and pride appear in this, that when miserable men do seek after God, instead of ascending higher than themselves as they ought to do, they measure him by their own carnal stupidity, and neglecting solid inquiry, fly off to indulge their curiosity in vain speculation. Hence, they do not conceive of him in the character in which he is manifested, but imagine him to be whatever their own rashness has devised. This abyss standing open, they cannot move one footstep without rushing headlong to destruction. With such an idea of God, nothing which they may attempt to offer in the way of worship or obedience can have any value in his sight, because it is not him they worship, but, instead of him, the dream and figment of their own heart.[15]

God is challenging us to give up our vain pursuits and prideful ambitions and clothe ourselves with humility, until our existence melts into the image of Jesus.

From the very onset of the Bible we recognize our dependence on God and God noticed our need to be around other people. Genesis 2:18, "The Lord God said, 'It is not good for the man to be alone. I will make a helper suitable for him.'" It's time to put our faith and trust in Someone greater than ourselves. I'm talking about complete surrender to the will of God. Surrender means to give oneself up into the power of another. Have we done that as Americans, or have we turned our backs

[15] John Calvin, *Institutes of the Christian Religion* (London: Reinolde Vvolf and Richarde Harisson, 1561), 46.

on the only One who can save us? To me the answer is clear. God is challenging us to give up our vain pursuits and prideful ambitions and clothe ourselves with humility, until our existence melts into the image of Jesus. Psalm 20:7 says, "Some trust in chariots, and some in horses; but we will remember the name of the Lord our God."

A. W. Tozer said:

> A generation of Christians reared among push buttons and automatic machines are impatient of slower and less direct methods of reaching their goals. We have been trying to apply machine-age methods to our relations with God. We read our chapter, have our short devotions, and rush away, hoping to make up for our deep inward bankruptcy by attending another gospel meeting or listening to another thrilling story told by a religious adventurer lately returned from afar. The tragic results of this spirit are all about us. Shallow lives, hollow religious philosophies, the preponderance of the element of fun in gospel meetings, the glorification of men, trust in religious externalities, quasi-religious fellowships, salesmanship methods, and the mistaking of dynamic personality for the power of the Spirit; these and such as these are the symptoms of an evil disease, a deep and serious malady of the soul. [16]

Have we replaced our dependence on God with the vanities of this life? All of our modern technologies still at best offer little in the way of lasting joy. Only undivided devotion to the Lord will satiate the longing soul with its deepest need. The more you rely on God, the more you recognize

Only undivided devotion to the Lord will satiate the longing soul with its deepest need.

[16] A. W. Tozer, *The Pursuit of God* (Harrisburg, PA: Christian Publications, 1948), 69.

your need for Him. The less you rely on Him, the less you think you need Him.

Prayerlessness is sin. We must keep the lines of communication open with God lest we stray away. I have met people who have once enjoyed sweet fellowship with Jesus but slowly began to drift from Him, allowing all kinds of sin to creep in until their idea of right and wrong was terribly skewed. It is amazing how quickly we stray away from God's ancient "boundary stones." What was supposed to never be removed has not only been removed but replaced with worthless idols.

When I was in high school I had a very terrifying dream. In my dream I was running outside, close to my grandparents' house. Suddenly I heard a sound in the sky like that of a jet flying through the air. I looked up in time to notice the skies split in two. I saw an angel with a trumpet in his hand and Jesus standing next to him. I fell to my knees and began to weep profusely. I looked into the eyes of Jesus and both saw, and felt, the pain my sinful lifestyle put Him through. I knew He was concerned for my spiritual well-being. I woke up sweating, and with tears streaming down my face, I bowed beside my bed and asked forgiveness for my sins. Every time I thought about the dream or tried relaying it to someone I would tear up. An indelible imprint of heaven was written upon my soul that day that I will never forget.

I had removed the boundary stones from my life. I had stopped praying, reading my Bible, and being a witness of any kind. By all outward appearances I was not a Christ follower. I would like to say that the dream changed me immediately, but it did not. Although, it was a constant reminder to me that Jesus was pursuing me. It also filled me with an awe and fear of God.

By the time my graduation from high school came around, so did my heart towards God. A couple months later I began to pursue Jesus. I started Bible school classes, began praying every day for at least an hour, oftentimes several hours, and worked in my church in whatever capacity they would allow.

Desperation

God desires to hear the cries out of a heart of desperation for Him. We must heed the instruction of Proverbs 3:5-6: "Trust in the Lord with all your heart, And lean not on your own understanding; In all your ways acknowledge Him, And He shall direct your paths." Desperation causes you to do what you would not normally do.

When I was in my early twenties I went on a forty-day fast. I honestly didn't even think I was going to make it through the fast. There were days that my body seemed to scream out for food and nourishment. I felt very faint and lightheaded. When I would walk up a flight of stairs I would have to hold onto the hand railing to keep from falling. I was desperate for God and was willing to put my body through the rigors of a fast to die to my own selfish ways so I could be alive in my spirit.

It is one thing to quote the Scripture about "man not living on bread alone, but by every word that proceeds out of the mouth of God," but it was a totally different thing to put it to the test. Many nights I shut myself in my room, turned on worship music, and poured my soul out to God. There were other nights, though, I couldn't keep my mind off of food. I dreamed of jumping out of my second-story window and limping down the road to a local barbeque place. I was constantly receiving offers from close friends to go out to eat with them.

I never realized how much my flesh craved earthly pleasures, but my spirit longed for deep connection with God.

I never realized how much my flesh craved earthly pleasures, but my spirit longed for deep connection with God. I thought the heavens would be quick to open to me in supernatural ways (i.e., amazing visions, awesome revelations, and third heaven experiences), but God ended up revealing Himself to me in the depths of my soul. He strengthened my resolve and gave me direction for my life. He made the crooked paths straight and caused doors of opportunity to open to me. I still believe that I'm seeing the fruits of my "wilderness experience." I am writing this to shed light on what it would take to cause us Christians to get desperate enough for God that we would do what seemed to be radical in order to bring the realities of heaven to earth.

There are many radical organizations around the world that are trying desperately to spread their message. Take for example the homosexual agenda. The reason the homosexual agenda has made such inroads into our culture is largely due to the fact that they have been active in every area of our modern world. They show up in everything from grassroots town hall meetings, to the biggest blockbusters in Hollywood, and all the way to Capitol Hill. The key is they have a burning agenda that is pushed by diehard adherents and activists that would give their life to spread this message. If they can spread their message with such fervor, we should be even more passionate about our eternal mandate!

When was the last time you stepped outside your comfort zone and did something bold for the Kingdom of God? I'm not trying to bring condemnation, but I am wanting...no, more than that...*God* is wanting to stir your spirit to lay hold of His heavenly treasures so we can press home the claims of God here on earth. How do we lay hold of the things of God? By getting desperate for them! Jesus said in Matthew 5:6, "...those who hunger and thirst after righteousness shall be filled."

Most Christians are so full of themselves that there is no room left for God. Do we actually think we are doing God a service by going to church on Sunday and that's it? Is this what the Christian life has been diluted down to...a measly two-hour service a week? The disciples would be appalled by our lack of devotion to the things of God!

Leonard Ravenhill said, "We live in a day of itching ears, but I have no commission from God to scratch them!"[17] Most people are okay with getting their spiritual ears scratched, but there is a remnant of hungry souls who are not satisfied with watered-down Gospel messages that cheapen grace and label holiness as legalism. True grace will always lead us away from sin. Titus 2:11-14 speaks about the effects of grace in our life:

> [11] For the grace of God has appeared, bringing salvation for all people, [12] training us to renounce ungodliness and worldly passions, and to live self-controlled, upright, and godly lives in the present age, [13] waiting for our blessed hope, the appearing of the glory of our great God and Savior Jesus Christ, [14] who gave himself for us to redeem us from all lawlessness and to purify for himself a people for his own possession who are zealous for good works (ESV).

There is a movement of Christ-followers that is emerging in the earth today who are coming back to the person of Jesus and the simplicity of pure devotion to Him.

There is a movement of Christ-followers that is emerging in the earth today who are coming back to the person of Jesus and the simplicity of pure devotion to Him.

We have to stir ourselves to go after Him (Jesus) and then go after them (the world)! They need to see a demonstration of the realities of heaven in their life! You need to make yourself available to God to be the instrument by which the demonstration can flow. If God's own Son used miracles to press home the claims of heaven here on earth, than we should never think that His plan in our time for mass evangelism is any different.

[17] Ravenhill, "Audio/Video Messages," http://www.ravenhill.org/mp3.htm.

We pray for open heavens but fail to realize that we are the answer to our own prayers! We have been made stewards of the mysteries of Christ! God sent us His Holy Spirit! We pray for open heavens without realizing that the Holy Spirit in us, and working through us, is the most powerful force in spreading the Good News! We are the temples of the Holy Ghost! We have been made into a habitation for His presence! While you are sitting and waiting on a sign from God, turn over to Acts 2, and realize your sign came two thousand years ago in an upper room! Now, our only correct response to God is, "HERE AM I, SEND ME!"

We pray for open heavens without realizing that the Holy Spirit in us, and working through us, is the most powerful force in spreading the Good News!

We Must Have Faith

God wants us to live an exciting and effective life. The Christian life without faith is like bread without yeast. Just like the bread is flat, Christianity without faith is boring. To have faith, there are two things I need to know about God:

1. God is eternally faithful to His Word.
2. God is eternally faithful to those who follow His Word.

Hebrews 11:1 says, "Now faith is the substance of things hoped for, the evidence of things not seen." Hope is the precursor to faith. It helps to prepare the way for faith, but we should never confuse it with faith. God is not moved simply by our hope; He is moved by our faith. Faith has its origins in the unseen realm, making it visible only to the spiritually observant.

Oftentimes we miss key moments of growth and breakthrough because we fail to realize the outstretched arm of our unseen God. God is not incapable or unwilling to display His wonders in our life. Proverbs 25:2 says, "It is the glory of God to conceal a thing: but the honour of kings is to search out a matter" (KJV). Faith searches out what has been hidden by God for us.

There is a perpetual order to the way God does things. That's why we have seasons. I'm never worried that summer is going to come during winter or that fall will take the place of spring. I have to believe that God is a good God because that is His nature. He never ceases to be good even when He is being just. It is in His goodness where we discover His glory.

Exodus 33:18-19 says, "And he said, 'Please, show me Your glory.' Then He said, 'I will make all My goodness pass before you, and I will proclaim the name of the Lord before you. I will be gracious to whom I will be gracious, and I will have compassion on whom I will have compassion.'"

Before we can release His glory we must experience His goodness. Moses returned from the mountain literally glowing from his encounter with God. The Israelites knew that he had a very special bond with God. Unfortunately, they failed to realize God wanted the same kind of relationship with them. When He tried to show them His favor they shrunk back in fear. God wanted to make them a kingdom of priests, but instead had to designate Aaron and his sons to be priests for them.

How often have we chosen to let somebody else approach God for us? Why not come to Him yourself? Why not discover for yourself that He is a good God? Why take somebody else's word for it?

If I'm not convinced that my faith releases His favor, then I will choose to live in the realm of unbelief.

In order to have faith in God, I must believe that I have found favor in His sight through righteousness. God made me righteous when I accepted the love and grace of Jesus Christ. Alone, I am nothing. But I can do all things through Christ who strengthens me. In Christ, my mind is renewed; I am a new creation. If I'm not convinced that my faith releases His favor, then I will choose to live in the realm of unbelief.

Luke 2:52 says, "And Jesus increased in wisdom and stature, and in favor with God and men." Jesus did nothing without seeing the Father do it first. In order to grow and be effective in our Christian life, it is necessary to see with spiritual eyes. We shouldn't wander aimlessly through life. What assignment has God given you today? Find out, and then get to work. James 2:17 says, "Faith without works is dead." Faith is not found camping out by past failures; nor is it found camping out by past accomplishments.

If we have distanced ourselves through a heart of unbelief, we will reap the bitter results that come with this stale approach to God.

Our level of faith is an excellent barometer of where our heart is with the Lord. If we are close to Him through faith, then we will naturally, effortlessly, begin to mirror the realities of His world in ours. Our devotion to Him will flow over into every aspect of our lives. If we have distanced ourselves through a heart of unbelief, we will reap the bitter results that come with this stale approach to God.

If we are not careful we can allow ourselves to become spiritually dull, but according to Hebrews 4:12, "the word of the Lord is living and active, sharper than any two-edged sword." There is nothing more embarrassing and potentially dangerous than watching an amateur wield a weapon that he has not been trained to use. The declination of our Christian foundation is becoming more and more prevalent as our world plunges deeper into darkness. Every day another so-called leader in the church is caught in a lie, gives into gross temptation, or shrinks back from speaking the truth in love.

God is looking for someone with faith who will have the prophetic edge to cut through the smokescreen of the enemy. As the "prince of the power of the air," the devil has polluted mainstream Christianity with pastors who care more about political correctness than the sanctity of God's Holy Word.

One of the most powerful verses in the Bible on combatting spiritual apathy is only three words long: "pray without ceasing" (1 Thessalonians 5:17). A vibrant heart, full of faith, is the result of intentional, unending communion with God.

Truths about Faith

- Faith sees what your physical eyes cannot see.
- Faith is expressed through creativity.
- Faith sees potential in the void.
- Without faith God is not pleased.
- Faith comes by hearing the Word of God.

The story of the valley of dry bones illustrates all of the above-mentioned truths about faith. Ezekiel walked through a valley of dry bones. God asked Ezekiel if the bones could live. Ezekiel saw dry bones, but God saw an army; He saw something of value in the bones that Ezekiel did not see. He knows that we are limited in our scope of vision. That is why He tells us to walk by faith, not by sight. When He speaks, our job is to listen and then correctly respond to Him.

I have noticed in my life that the actualization of faith comes oftentimes after my obedience. People that ask for God to perform a miracle first, and then declare their belief, are terribly mistaken. Instead they should meditate on the Word, thereby learning to hear God's voice, and then ask God to teach them His ways. Then they would come to a greater understanding of the nature and timing of God.

A vibrant heart, full of faith, is the result of intentional, unending communion with God.

There is not a famine of the Word of the Lord in the land, but there is a "famine of the hearing of the Word of the Lord" (Amos 8:11). We must intake the Word much like a cow intakes the grass, or the cud. It chews the cud, and then swallows it, only to regurgitate it back up again. It does this four times, because it has four different stomachs to help process the food. If the cow does not eat its food this way, it will not be able to produce milk properly.

As Christians it is necessary to meditate on the Word of God or else we will not be able to nourish ourselves properly; and even worse, we will not be able to "rightly divide the word of truth" for other people. This requires devotion to the Scriptures, "line upon line and precept upon precept." Joshua 1:8 says, "This Book of the Law shall not depart from your mouth, but you shall meditate on it day and night, so that you may be careful to do according to all that is written in it. For then you will make your way prosperous, and then you will have good success" (ESV).

Faith comes whenever you can look at a hopeless situation and find hope, whenever you can look at devastation and see restoration, and when you are sick in your body, but you know a Great Physician who has the power to heal. Ezekiel was looking down the barrel of a hopeless situation. The good news was that the God of all hope was in his midst.

Even though God's heart goes out to those in need, it does not mean He automatically responds to their need. He responds to His Word lived out through a life of faith. Ezekiel prophesied the Word of the Lord over the bones and then they stood up and became a vast army.

Sometimes we get faith and hope mixed up. Hope always looks to the future: someday God will heal me. Faith pulls the reality of what is happening in His world into our world. A. W. Tozer said in his book, *The Knowledge of the Holy*, "it's when earth is confronted with heaven...."[18] When is the last time you confronted your situation with the reality of heaven? Many times our prayers are statements of unbelief that reinforce our problems instead of proclamations of faith that dissolve our problems.

God is looking for just one person, one person with faith. James 5:16 says, "The prayer of a righteous man is powerful and effective." Anyone can burn in a crowd. Who will burn by themselves? The difference between boiling and hot water is one degree. The boiling point of water is 212 degrees Fahrenheit. That produces steam that can move a locomotive. You can be burned at 211 degrees, but it takes that extra degree to move things. Oftentimes we stop in our convenience, but faith is only realized in inconvenience. I've got to press past what is obvious to find what He has hidden *for* me, not *from* me. Your darkest moment in life may just be your greatest moment to find promotion.

Your darkest moment in life may just be your greatest moment to find promotion.

Adversity

Adversity is something we all try to avoid, but sometimes it is unavoidable. Jesus even warned us that "perilous times were coming." He said in Matthew 5:10-12, "Blessed are those who are persecuted for righteousness sake, For theirs is the kingdom of heaven. Blessed are you when they revile and persecute you, and say all kinds of evil against you falsely for My sake. Rejoice and be exceedingly glad, for great is your reward in heaven, for so they persecuted the prophets who were before you."

It is our privilege to experience suffering. If Jesus learned obedience through the things He suffered, then who are we to think that we will be exempt?

---

[18] A. W. Tozer, *Knowledge of the Holy* (New York: Harper & Row, 1961), 2.

In Philippians 3:10 Paul said, "That I may know him, and the power of his resurrection, and the fellowship of his sufferings, being made conformable unto his death" (KJV). We love the first part of that verse, but cringe at the last part. How many times have we been willing to suffer with Christ? We may have prayed a prayer similar to Paul's, but hoped it would never be answered.

When we get to heaven I believe we are going to get a glimpse of some amazing men and women who suffered greatly for their faith. They will be amongst those in Revelation 6:10 who call out to the Lord and "cry with a loud voice, saying, 'How long, O Lord, holy and true, dost thou not judge and avenge our blood on them that dwell on the earth?'" (KJV).

Chapter 6

The Voice of One

George Whitefield said, "I have just put my soul as a blank in the hand of Jesus, My Redeemer, and desired Him to write on it what He pleases. I know it will be His image."[19]

George Whitefield said, "I have just put my soul as a blank in the hand of Jesus, My Redeemer, and desired Him to write on it what He pleases. I know it will be His image."

Whenever I was in high school I had to take a home economics class. One project we were given was taking home a battery-operated baby. It was supposed to be a fairly accurate simulation of what it would be like to care for an actual baby. Instead it was a nightmare in the making. From the moment I took the baby home until its battery finally failed (Thank You, Jesus!), it would not stop crying. I tried putting the fake bottle in its mouth, and that did not work. I tried rocking it, and that did not work. I made sure I had its head

---

[19] George Whitefield quote reported in Josiah Hotchkiss Gilbert, *Dictionary of Burning Words of Brilliant Writers* (1895), p. 543.

supported when I held it, and that did not work. No matter what I tried to do, the baby would not be quiet.

Now I know what you might be thinking: "Man, if this guy can't even take care of a battery-operated baby, he will never be able to care for a baby of his own!" I want to prove to you that I am worthy of being a father someday. Even my mom, who had raised two kids on her own, was so stressed out by this thing that she made me call my teacher and ask if I could just take the battery out of its back. My teacher would not let me, insisting that all that was needed was a little loving care. So for the next few hours the baby cried nonstop. Finally I reached my boiling point. I grabbed a huge comforter off my bed and began wrapping the doll up to at least muffle the sound. I then threw it in the closet.

Eventually the battery died and the pleasant sound of silence filled the air. The next day I took the baby back to my teacher and she discovered a defect in the electronics of the baby. She gave me a passing grade, even though I felt I deserved the Medal of Honor!

The Testimony of John

It's amazing how much sound one voice can make. In John 1:19-28, we read the story of one such voice that shook the heavens and the earth with the call of, "Repent, for the kingdom of heaven is at hand!"

> 19 And this is the testimony of John, when the Jews sent
> priests and Levites from Jerusalem to ask him, "Who are
> you?" 20 He confessed, and did not deny, but confessed,
> "I am not the Christ." 21 And they asked him, "What
> then? Are you Elijah?" He said, "I am not." "Are you the
> Prophet?" And he answered, "No." 22 So they said to him,
> "Who are you? We need to give an answer to those who
> sent us. What do you say about yourself?" 23 He said, "I

am the voice of one crying out in the wilderness, 'Make straight the way of the Lord,' as the prophet Isaiah said."

[24] (Now they had been sent from the Pharisees.) [25] They asked him, "Then why are you baptizing, if you are neither the Christ, nor Elijah, nor the Prophet?" [26] John answered them, "I baptize with water, but among you stands one you do not know, [27] even he who comes after me, the strap of whose sandal I am not worthy to untie." [28] These things took place in Bethany across the Jordan, where John was baptizing. (ESV)

John had a testimony. His testimony moved him to a place of action. Our experience with God should lead us to compel others to encounter God. John had a mandate given to him from God to be a prophetic voice, preparing people's hearts and calling them to attention, because the great King was in their midst and they didn't even recognize it.

Today you have a testimony, if indeed you are saved. You have an amazing story of how God "has delivered you from the power of darkness, and has translated you into the Kingdom of His dear Son" (Colossians 1:13). You have a testimony of being spiritually blind, but now suddenly receiving your sight. You can testify to the fact that you are not the same person you used to be when you walked according to the prince of the power of the air.

Something amazing and significant has happened! You now have joy, peace, and a sense of forgiveness. The heaviness that used to weigh your heart down is now all of a sudden lifted, and you feel freedom for the first time. The Spirit of the Lord is present, granting you liberty. We dare not hold back our voices from declaring the wonderful deeds of our awesome God to our generation.

Be an Original

I want you to know God is not looking for another you. I've heard it said "that everybody is born an original, but most people die copies." He created your intellect, your personality, your skill sets, and your voice for His purposes. He didn't make you so you could be rich, famous, and successful. You may someday be rich, famous, and successful, but use that platform all the more to bring God glory through your life.

The disciples were known as "the poor ones." They were pinned as "uneducated men who had been with Jesus." They lacked the pedigree and the religious prowess that the Pharisees carried. Since the Pharisees rejected Jesus, Jesus rejected them and chose fishermen. He chose the foolish and despised things of the world to confound the wise.

The disciples became God's voice echoed everywhere from the cities to the synagogues, from the Sanhedrin to the Samaritans, and from Jerusalem to the uttermost parts of the world. The more persecution came to try and break the back of this newfound religion, the more strength it gathered. The more the world tried to silence it, the louder the voice grew. One voice turned into a multitude of voices, all declaring the same message.

Imagine if John the Baptist said, "I don't feel like being a voice, because who would want to listen to me anyway?". What if he would have spent his life living within the comfortable confines of his hometown instead of going through his time of preparation in the wilderness? Oh, how many of us have chosen the easy way out? How many of us have lacked the courage to speak the truth even if we were the only ones talking?

Break the Silence

It was four hundred years of silence between John and the other prophets. How many people had God called during those four hundred years to be His mouthpiece, but nothing was said? Countless generations passed by during that time with only the writings of previous prophets to suffice their inward cries for a demonstration of God's redemption to come. Some undoubtedly died without hearing of such an amazing God.

We must realize that we may be the only thing that separates people from standing before a holy, just God. God allowed Jesus to go through what He did not deserve so we could have what we do not deserve. That is the power of the love of God. If we think that we won't be held accountable for how we represented His love to other people, think again. If we think that unbelievers won't be held accountable for their own sins before God, we need to think again.

God allowed Jesus to go through what He did not deserve so we could have what we do not deserve.

Revelation 20:12 says, "And I saw the dead, small and great, stand before God; and the books were opened: and another book was opened, which is *the book* of life: and the dead were judged out of those things which were written in the books, according to their works" (KJV).

May that motivate us to snatch people from the fires of an eternity separated from God and cause us to introduce them to the unspeakable joys of knowing Jesus. Jesus declared in Matthew 11:12, "…from the days of John the Baptist until now, the kingdom of heaven was suffering violence and the violent take it by force." It's time for us to call people to aggressively pursue the things of God, "to cast off the weights and sins that so easily set us back and run with endurance the race that has been marked out before us" (Hebrews 12:1).

We have a responsibility to God, unbelievers, other Christians, and the great cloud of witnesses that have gone before us. Not only are unsaved people watching our lives, but other believers are also watching us, especially those who are new Christians. They need an accurate display of New Testament Christianity. They don't need some frail, anemic, diluted portrayal of watered-down faith. They need people who are firebrands, burning with a prophetic message of the enduring hope that only comes through relationship with Jesus. They need to see us being bold about our witness, and equally as bold about approaching God's throne room.

A Match Made in Heaven

There needs to be a balance between deep fellowship with God and passionate, Holy Spirit-led evangelism. We must not represent one without the other. They are married, in the same way that the Word and the Spirit are conjoined. They work in sync with one another. They depend on one another. "Faith without works is dead," and works without faith quickly become cold and ineffective. As Timothy followed in the footsteps of his spiritual father, Paul, may we be an example to those following us.

We have many that have gone before us, preparing a way for us to walk in. If not for them our roads might look more like a jungle than a pathway. They were the ones who cleared out the debris through their own blood, sweat, and tears. We owe them a life lived in holy abandon to God. The promises they worked towards can only be fully realized through us. We must not drop the baton else we short-circuit their reward that will only come through our obedience.

Of course they will receive their reward in heaven at the judgment seat of Christ, but their complete earthly inheritance depends in part on our faithfulness. With this in mind I urge you to live your life with holy conviction. Don't leave anything to chance. Be intentional in prayer. Be intentional in study. Be intentional in evangelism. Be intentional in loving other believers.

Be intentional in prayer. Be intentional in study. Be intentional in evangelism. Be intentional in loving other believers.

How are you going to reach your generation? How did John reach his generation? John 1:19-20 says, "And this is the testimony of John, when the Jews sent priests and Levites from

Jerusalem to ask him, 'Who are you?' He confessed, and did not deny, but confessed, 'I am not the Christ.'"

First his confession was right about who he was. We do not reach our generation by lying to them about our own abilities. John had a following of people. People came to him from all over, just to hear his words. Religious leaders came and even Herod came to hear from John.

An Unlikely Candidate

The interesting thing about John's appearance and speech was that he wasn't traditional in any sense of the word. He didn't fit into people's idea of what a preacher should look and talk like. He was dressed in stylish camel's hair. His hair was long and probably unkempt looking. He ate locusts and wild honey.

He didn't preach in a synagogue, but out in the open air. He wasn't trained by the Pharisees, but in the school of the prophets out in the wilderness. Everything about him was different than the usual pattern of a minister in that time and with their set of customs. So why did people come from all around just to hear this man speak?

I think this answer lies in John's statement about himself, "He said, 'I am the voice of one crying out in the wilderness, "Make straight the way of the Lord,"' as the prophet Isaiah said" (John 1:23). His call was not from men, like that of the Pharisees, but his call was from God. He was sovereignly chosen by God and prophesied about hundreds of years prior to his "public appearing to Israel."

He was not just any voice crying out in the wilderness; He was God's handpicked voice coming at the appointed time to prepare the way for the Messiah. Wow! What a responsibility! I believe from a very young age John knew what he was called to do. He knew his training in the wilderness was pivotal to the coming of the Messiah. He wasn't just any voice—he was a specific voice for that moment in time.

I believe as a child of God you are not just any voice, but you are a specific voice. I just now received a phone call from a friend who shared a testimony of a word I spoke a couple years ago to a young man in ministry. I had never met him before, but I felt impressed by God to tell him that God had called him to be an evangelist. It was this simple word that helped launch him into his next phase of life. Within a few months he made the decision to move to another state and pursue this calling.

I was a specific voice God used to direct the footsteps of this young man. What if I had not spoken up and left it to chance? What if I would have let fear keep me from sharing the word of the Lord to that young man? I would have been called to account for what I did not say. Someday you will be called to account for what you did not say in this life.

One voice may reach a community, but multiple voices will reach nations.

Paul said in Romans 1:16, "For I am not ashamed of the Gospel of Jesus Christ, for it is the power of God unto salvation to everyone who believes, to the Jew first, then the Greek." We need to lift up our voices and imitate Romans 10:18, "But I say, have they not heard? Yes indeed: Their sound has gone out to all the earth, And their words to the ends of the world." May our voices be lifted up in one accord as an anthem that will spread to the ends of the world. One voice may reach a community, but multiple voices will reach nations.

The Voice and the Word

John was a voice, but Jesus is the Word. John's voice prepared the way for the Word to come. John said, "I'm not the Christ," I'm just a voice. We are not the Word, but we must allow the Word to anoint our words.

Remember, it is the Lord's Word that spoke the world into existence.

It is His Word that has stood the test of time, persecution, and the brink of utter annihilation, to be preserved for future generations.

It is His Word that confused our words at the tower of Babel.

It is His Word that spoke to Noah to be a "preacher of righteousness" and prepare an ark for the saving of his family; and not only his family, but future generations.

It is His Word that called Abram, Abraham, and made him "the father of many nations."

It is His Word that spoke out of a burning bush to Moses and commanded Him to be a deliverer to the enslaved Israelites.

It is His Word that made the Israelites cross through water not once, but twice.

It is His Word that subdues foreign armies, thwarts the plans of the wicked, raises up Godly leaders, shuts the mouth of lions, and saves from the edge of the sword.

It is His Word that was spoken through His holy prophets long ago, proclaiming justice to the oppressed and freedom to the captives.

It was His Word that prophesied the coming of the Messiah and the end of the age.

It was His Word that established His church, so that the gates of hell would not prevail against it.

It is His Word that has stood the test of time, persecution, and the brink of utter annihilation, to be preserved for future generations.

His Word is eternal. His Word sustains all that we see, and gives life to our mortal bodies.

Without the foundation of His Word in our hearts, our words will be lifeless. John had a testimony from God. May God be the One Who validates our voice and gives us a testimony worth hearing.

Chapter 7

The Man God Chooses

"A man with God is always in the majority." [20]

—John Knox

As the people of God, the church, we are never the minority, because Jesus is with us. We are referred to as His body. We have Him attached to us wherever we go. None other of God's creation has this privilege. His thoughts become our actions. We should be set in motion by the slightest inclinations of His mind, just like a pitcher knows to release a ball when his arm is fully extended.

It is no wonder that the enemy wants to pollute our holy union with God. He wants to malign the church and cause it to be a byword amongst the nations. Furthermore, he wants the church to question its own validity. I do not know how many times I have heard the church blasted by those in the church. Jesus said a nation divided against its self cannot stand. I just finished reading a magazine article entitled "Forget Church,

[20] John Knox quote, Inscription on Reformation monument, Geneva, Switzerland. "A man with God is always in the majority," by John Knox, BrainyQuote®, www.brainyquote.com/quotes/quotes/j/johnknox194151.html.

How do I show God that my heart is completely His, that I am a man worth choosing? I follow after Him with all my heart.

Follow Jesus."[21] Although the article had some good points, the thought of forgetting the church to follow Jesus is absurd. How are you going to forget about His body and His bride? This is not some title we have self-righteously given ourselves. He refers to us as His body, and likewise, He refers to us as His bride. No husband wants his bride to be ridiculed by others. He will defend her. Make sure you are on His side.

Psalm 4:3: "But know that the Lord hath set apart him that is godly for Himself…" (KJV). What an awesome thought; that the God of the universe would choose to handpick a person for Himself. Think about that for a second…that He would set us apart for His own delight. I had a dream one night that I was staring over a casket with a few other men standing around me. Our intention was to raise the man in the casket from the dead. As we prayed, the man in the casket sat straight up, looked me in the eyes, and said, "God hates me, but He is pleased with you." He then lay back down in the casket and I woke up. I realized the man in the casket was my "old nature." God was reassuring me through the dream that I was on the right path.

Galatians 2:20 says, "I am crucified with Christ: nevertheless I live; yet not I, but Christ liveth in me: and the life which I now live in the flesh I live by the faith of the Son of God, who loved me, and gave himself for me" (KJV).

Mere words never fool God into thinking something that is not true about us. He is always looking for someone who has forsaken earthly pleasures to pursue heavenly pleasures. Let your delight be in Him and you will never be put to shame. How do

[21] Andrew Sullivan. 2012. "Forget the Church, Follow Jesus," *Newsweek,* April 9.

I show God that my heart is completely His, that I am a man worth choosing? I follow after Him with all my heart.

I recently witnessed to a man who referred to himself as an atheist. I told him that if he truly sought God with all his heart he would find Him. I then told him that after he discovered God was real, then he could either accept or reject having a relationship with Him. Atheists exist only because they have not truly sought the Lord. That is why God refers to them as fools. Only a fool would deny his opportunity to know his Maker. God promises to make Himself known to those who are in genuine pursuit of Him.

Moses was a man whom God set apart for a specific task. He was a man with a heart for God, but this was not always the case. His road to revelation started off bumpy, to say the least. He escaped the fate of death as a baby, even though those who would have been his contemporaries did not. He was raised in the house of the very one who issued this demonic slaughter of innocent lives. God has always and will always secure His remnant in the earth.

God has always and will always secure His remnant in the earth.

Even after Moses killed an Egyptian for beating a fellow Hebrew, God still had a plan for him. Moses could run away from the most powerful man on earth, but could never outrun the One who sits enthroned on high.

Let's fast-forward forty years. Moses has been a sheepherder in the land of Midian. He has a wife, a child, and a family that loves him. His life is simple, but the scars of his past failures remain. Not only did he kill a man, but his whole race of people is in cruel bondage under Pharaoh. He must have thought, "I could never go back and show myself to Pharaoh without an army backing me up." Finally the fateful day came when God called to him from a bush that was on fire. At first Moses rejected this mission from God. He questioned his calling. He tried to convince God to find someone else.

When we yield to our fallen nature we have a tendency to shirk responsibility. Listen to what William Booth had to say about this subject:

> 'Not called!' did you say? 'Not heard the call,' I think you should say. Put your ear down to the Bible, and hear him bid you go and pull sinners out of the fire of sin. Put your ear down to the burdened, agonized heart of humanity, and listen to its pitiful wail for help. Go stand by the gates of hell, and hear the damned entreat you to go to their father's house and bid their brothers and sisters, and servants and masters not to come there. And then look Christ in the face, whose mercy you have professed to obey, and tell him whether you will join heart and soul and body and circumstances in the march to publish his mercy to the world."[22]

If that does not motivate to reach this generation, then you might need to check your spiritual pulse.

Moses eventually softened his heart and accepted this mission. I think ever since Moses saw the burning bush, he longed for a similar experience with God. He could have let things get in the way of pursuing God, but he knew he could not allow his fear to paralyze him.

He had come to know the Lord in such a profound and personal way. I think his heart ached when he was away from God. Moses spent years running away from his past, feeling dead inside, but in a millisecond…standing in front of the burning bush, face-to-face with the presence of God…he realized, this is what I was made for, and I'm never going back to the way I used to be.

You would think that volumes of books could be written about the first forty years of Moses' life, but God only designates

---

[22] William Booth quote. "Mission Quotes," To Every Tribe, https://www.toeverytribe.com/missionquotes.

the first few chapters in Exodus to show us Moses' tainted past. This is the way God chooses to treat us. He leaves us with a faint reminder of our past sins as proof of what we have been brought out of. He does not bring them to the surface and taunt us for the bad decisions we used to make. Instead, God redirects our focus to our present standing with Him.

The man God chooses will lose his own will in the will of God!

The man God chooses will lose his own will in the will of God! Moses' life became one with his heavenly Father. Jesus, in John 15, prayed that we would be one with each other and one with Him. We have been hidden with God in Christ. Where is the best place to be lost? The answer is, in God.

The man God chooses will stand before God. Psalm 24:3, "Who may ascend into the hill of the Lord? Or who may stand in His holy place?" What a challenge! What an invitation! God wants to position us in His holy place. He wants us to look from the perspective of heaven. This reminds me of Peter, James, and John getting to be with Jesus on the Mount of Transfiguration. They were in such awe, because of what they had just seen, they did not even know how to respond. When we see Him in His glory, the most appropriate response is silence.

If I am aware that His anointing is on me and I walk in it, I will live like nothing is impossible for him who believes. Doubt and unbelief will take a back seat to courage and faith.

The Call

When I first started out in ministry, I worked at a gas station. I heard God's voice very clearly say, "If you will obey Me, I will show you a miracle this week." That Sunday, a few of us prayed for a man confined to a wheelchair. That man stood up and walked! The only thing that limits what God can do through us is us. He has chosen to partner with man to reach man. We must believe that through Him all things are possible.

To the sheep, the Shepherd's call is unmistakable. When we are in His care His voice becomes very familiar to us. We know that He intends us no harm or ill will. He shows us time and time again that He is willing to put Himself in harm's way just to protect us. Jesus said of all the Father had given Him, He had lost none, except for Judas. Why did the other disciples remain so faithful and Judas did not? I can only speculate, but I assume they came so near to Jesus that their very identities merged into His. They became one with Him in spirit and mission. Oh, what amazing things God could accomplish through those who become one with Him! The whole course of our lives would be set in motion by the heartbeat of heaven!

There are gifts that He gives us that may seem unimpressive, but through His Spirit those gifts become mighty in our hands.

Jesus, teach us Your ways that we may instruct others! As we put our hands to the plow, show us Your unseen hand in motion! Release heavenly rain over Your fields and vineyards, and supply us with the right resources to present to You an abundant harvest in due season! We know all we have and all we will receive comes from You! Amen.

The man God chooses will use what God has placed in his hands. What do I mean? There are gifts that He gives us that may seem unimpressive, but through His Spirit those gifts become mighty in our hands.

Take for instance Moses' staff. What was so impressive about a staff? Why would a staff being held over a river cause the waters to roll back and stand in a huge heap so that the Israelites could cross over on dry ground? Why would a sling and a rock in David's hand be able to take down a monstrosity like Goliath? In our hands they seem useless, but God uses the foolish things in the world to confound the wise. "The weapons of our warfare are not carnal, but are mighty in God..." (2 Corinthians 10:4).

Without Holiness

The man God chooses courageously guards his convictions. He flees temptation; he does not flirt with it.

Years ago a visiting pastor told a story at my home church that stuck with me. As a freshman football player in high school he happened to be good enough to play on the varsity squad. At the big homecoming game he played really well, helping his team secure a victory over their opponent. After the game was over, his older football "buddies" drove him around town, doing victory laps. He did not think his night could get any better.

What happened next caught him off guard. His "buddies" stopped the vehicle at a park, got out of the car, and ran off into the night. Within a few minutes the back car door opened and a girl crawled in the backseat with him. Without any hesitation the girl began to take her top off. Most unbelievers would consider this the perfect ending to a fairy-tale night; but he wasn't an unbeliever. He was raised in church and loved God.

His escape from the car reminds me of Joseph's escape from Potiphar's wife. He didn't even try to negotiate with sin for a second. He flung open the door, jumped out of the car, and took off. In that moment the only thought that raced through his mind was, "What if Jesus came back and I would have been caught with my pants down?"[23] His fear of the Lord saved him from making a terrible mistake that could have haunted him for the rest of his life.

---

[23] From a sermon Pastor Gary Grogan preached at First Assembly of God in Fairfield, Illinois.

James 4:7 says to "submit to the Lord, resist the devil and he will flee from you." Too many Christians waste their time rebuking the enemy, when all that is really required is submission to God. They do all this having already settled it in their minds to yield to their flesh once again. Why not submit to the One who has already made a public spectacle of the enemy and brought him to an open shame? We need to flee youthful lusts and be captivated by the "Desire of all Nations!" We need to fall in love with the "Lover of our Souls!"

He wants to awaken men and women who are full of His Spirit, firmly established in His Word, and who don't negotiate with sin.

Many Christians put themselves in situations they should never be in, compromising their integrity and character. Temptation sparks intrigue, and intrigue leads to lust. If lust isn't dealt with at its infancy stage, it can plunge your heart into full-blown rebellion.

So what is God's recipe for recapturing the attention of a lust-driven generation? He wants to awaken men and women who are full of His Spirit, firmly established in His Word, and who don't negotiate with sin. That is the foundation of living a discipled life. No matter if it's popular or if people think we are crazy, we are called to live holy lives.

Shaking Things Up

Matthew 11:7: "As they departed, Jesus began to say to the multitudes concerning John: 'What did you go out into the wilderness to see? A reed shaken by the wind?'" The people thought John was crazy, but Jesus declared him to be a prophet. A man with unshakable convictions has a way of shaking other people up.

In several different passages the Bible refers to us as priests. A priest was held to a higher standard than the rest of the world.

The people of Israel depended on the priest remaining set apart for the service of the Lord. If the priest was not pure before the Lord, then he suffered a terrible fate: death. The animals people brought to be sacrificed were of excellent quality. They were the best of their stock. Imagine the priest offering an animal that was more acceptable in God's sight than the priest was.

Imagine us, the living sacrifices, offering ourselves in an unworthy fashion to God. The world, too often, is left hanging by a thread over the torments of hell, while we shuffle our feet, refusing to crawl up on heaven's altar. It is time for us to challenge the status quo of our worship. Let us refuse to be nominal, subpar Christians! It is time to push the envelope of apathy and enter into the realm of the apostolic!

Sometimes God's plans are put into motion by a little commotion. Since the grain of this world runs against the grain of His world, we are oftentimes left with no other choice but steadfast opposition to this world's ungodly laws and unjust legislations. God's laws are perfect, but man's laws can be tainted. We need to be willing to join our voices with the disciples and say, "Judge for yourself, is it better for us to obey God, or man?"

It is time to push the envelope of apathy and enter into the realm of the apostolic!

The second floor of the National Museum of American History in Washington, DC, contains an eighteenth-century Bible owned by Thomas Jefferson. It has precisely cut-out sections of Scripture. According to the writings of Thomas Jefferson he was excavating the "diamonds" from the "dunghill."[24] He referred to Jesus' words in red as the diamonds and the rest of the New Testament as a dunghill. What a sad commentary

[24] Quote taken from an eighteenth-century Bible owned by Thomas Jefferson on the second floor of the National Museum of American History in Washington, DC. "Jefferson Bible," Wikipedia, http://en.wikipedia.org/wiki/Jefferson_Bible

coming from a founding father and president. He did not see the whole Bible as inspired by God.

Sometimes on my lunch break, a couple of friends from work and I, go to a local bus stop and witness to people waiting for the bus. I get a chance to meet many people that hold the same view toward the inspiration of Scripture. They tell me that imperfect men wrote the Bible so it has to be full of mistakes.

Not too long ago, I spoke with a guy who told me that he had read all through the Bible but just could not believe the miracles Jesus did or the claims He made about Himself. He said that God would have to show up and do something unbelievable for him to believe. I then pointed to a tree and said, "Creation is proof enough of His existence. There is only One who can create and sustain life!" The thought that the world was conceived and set in motion by a random unrelated set of anomalies is absurd. Just like magnificent paintings that adorn an art gallery, His handiwork is all around and should be a constant reminder to us that there is an intelligent, loving Creator.

We must stick strong to our convictions! We cannot be moved even if everything else around us is shifting and changing. The world is never without change, and that is the reason people in the world need to see your resilience in keeping with the ancient principles and practical application of the Holy Scriptures.

The "Real" You

So, what is the "real" you? There are con artists out there getting paid big money to help people find their "inner self." I just read a popular magazine with an article about "finding your inner Jesus." Every product you buy in the store has a warning label on it. Allow the Bible to be your warning label that helps you sift through the garbage to find the gold.

Immerse yourself in the God of the Bible and you will discover who you are in Him and why He created you.

Any time you hear some self-help guru trying to push their spiritual concepts on you, run away. Do not give them even a second of your time, unless it is to bring correction on their false idea of Jesus. All they want to do is give you a manageable-sized god that you can hide away in your pocket and pull him out at your convenience. Instead, immerse yourself in the God of the Bible and you will discover who you are in Him and why He created you.

We need to define the perception of what is "real" and what is "religious." For the sake of appearing "real" to the world…we have approached God flippantly. In Hebrews 9, Paul tells us that the high priest would enter the Holy of Holies to offer a sacrifice on behalf of the people. This was a very serious sacrifice in the eyes of God. The priest had to make sure to go through the proper procedures and protocol before he ever entered the Holy of Holies. If he did not approach God correctly there were very dire consequences. We should be overjoyed because Jesus went into the Holy of Holies once for all, and made the ultimate sacrifice.

Many people use this as an excuse to come before God half-heartedly. If anything, this should cause us to approach Him with complete humility and a heart of repentance. It is a new fad to preach revival before repentance, but God will not go against His Holy Word just to satisfy man's rebellious emotions. There is only one way to be filled with a greater sense of His presence. Jesus explained it in Matthew 5:6 in His Sermon on the Mount: "…those who hunger and thirst after righteousness shall be filled."

We cannot talk about being hungry and thirsty for more of God and then neglect right living. Even though Jesus paid the price for our sin, He will always instruct us to "go and sin no more."

Even though Jesus paid the price for our sin, He will always instruct us to "go and sin no more."

We ridicule people who dress modestly, choose not to watch certain things, and call them "religious." The people who are edgier, have their own set of rules, and exchange God's Word for new-age teachings are considered "real."

Where did we get this? Mixing the spiritual with the fleshly does not make you a Christian. Real Christians try to live holy lives. They are not perfect, and they understand that, but they don't use their weaknesses as a crutch to do or say whatever they want. They do not ignore certain moral guardrails that are put up for their protection.

Real Christians reach the culture by going with the grain of God's Kingdom. They don't have to throw their standards out the window or trample on sound teaching to try to make disciples.

They use certain outlets in the culture, without being controlled or manipulated by them. Everything is done for God's glory, to accomplish His agenda.

Real Christians submit to their authorities. They do not mock them; they pray for them. They invite correction when needed, and desire to be discipled. They welcome mentors, spiritual fathers and mothers.

The Real Christian, the man God chooses…takes up his cross daily, because to him, it is not only a sign of dying to self, but living for God.

Chapter 8

Suffering Servants Make Good Soldiers

I want to begin this chapter with a poem that I wrote a couple of years ago:

The Suffering Servant
by Darrin Vaughan

There was a lot of commotion that day,
As a man that some would say
Bent the rules of religion, and did things His own way.
Some cried, "Crucify," while His mother wept and sighed.
The verdict was given and the nails were driven,
And out of the hands that healed, His blood did spill onto the barren ground.
Our shame was atoned for that day by His pain.
The thief and the centurion heard heaven's call,
As others mocked, and tried to make Him drink wine mixed with gall.
He refused this worldly temptation, not giving in to a temporary sensation,

And He looked for strength from His Father above, longing for that reassuring love.
But instead of gazing upon the sin that was placed upon by the sons of men,
The Father turned away in tears, even though He had never before in thirty-three years.
Jesus was on His own, you see, as He cried to His Father, "Why have you forsaken Me?"
Then darkness descended from on high,
And it seemed that the enemy had won the fight.
The ground began to pound, and the veil was ripped in two
As Jesus prepared the way for all to become new.
King James says, "He gave up the ghost,"
And even though He could have, He never left that old rugged post.
The soldiers came with eyes of stone, carrying a wooden mallet to break their bones.
And coming to Jesus they could see, that He had already slipped into eternity.
As blood and water poured from His side,
The deeds of humanity could no longer hide.
The King of the Jews was dead, and all of His disciples had fled.
Joseph and Nicodemus were the only ones to retrieve His body.
They wrapped him in linen and this became His womb,
So they placed Him inside their open tomb.
They rolled a stone in front of the tomb, closing out the light to this once empty room.
For three days the tomb remained silent;
The Kingdom of heaven had suffered violence.
Now it was time to be taken by force by the One who had finished His course.
His eyes of fire, His feet like bronze, now wrapped in white, the grave clothes gone.
The stone was rolled away that day,
As He emerged from a crypt designed for decay.

Mortality has dawned immortality, and the corruptible has
been clothed with incorruption,
God not seeing fit to pardon the interruption!
O death, where is thy sting? O grave, where is thy victory?
You've been swallowed up by the God who breathes
stars from afar
And by the Son, the original morning star.
Let the peoples of the earth now say, "Salvation is here for us
today!"

Our suffering servant, Jesus, didn't go to the cross just to start a religion; He went to the cross to finish a war. The war started with Satan and a third of the angels being tossed out of heaven. Satan knew he couldn't stand up to God, so he went after His creation. There was one little detail he didn't account for: the cross. Colossians 2:15 says, "Having disarmed principalities and powers, He made a public spectacle of them, triumphing over them in it."

Our suffering servant, Jesus, didn't go to the cross just to start a religion; He went to the cross to finish a war.

It was at the cross that we get the image of two different kinds of soldiers. One group of them was casting lots for His robe, while another soldier was cut to the heart by what he had just witnessed. Matthew 27:54 records this story: "So when the centurion and those with him, who were guarding Jesus, saw the earthquake and the things that had happened, they feared greatly, saying, 'Truly this was the Son of God!'" While a vast majority of people fall into the first category of soldiers, there are "a remnant" that have seen their suffering Savior on the cross and have confessed, "This truly is the Son of God."

Second Timothy 2:3-4: "Share in suffering as a good soldier of Christ Jesus. To please the recruiter, no one serving as a soldier gets entangled in the concerns of everyday life" (CSB). It is our great privilege to share in our Lord's suffering.

Charles Spurgeon said this about soldiers:

> "There is no glory in being a featherbed soldier, a man bedecked with gorgeous medals, but never beautified by a scar, or ennobled by a wound. All that you ever hear of such a soldier is that his spurs jingle on the pavement as he walks. There is no history for this carpet knight. He is just a dandy. He never smelled gunpowder in battle in his life. If he did, he fetched out his cologne to kill the offensive odor. Oh, if we could be wise enough to choose, even were as wise as the Lord Himself, we would choose the troubles which He has appointed to us, and we would not spare ourselves a single pang."[25]

From Clown to Clone

I went to school with a guy who enlisted in the Marines. Before he went to the Marines, he was a cutup, the class clown, the goof-off, and the funny guy. He was a bit unorganized in his appearance. He didn't care if his shirt was a little wrinkled and not stuffed into his pants. He was your typical American teenager, who was about to collide with an exceptional branch of the military. Something had to give, and that something wasn't going to be the military.

I remember visiting him when he came back from the Marines for a short furlough. He was no longer a disheveled looking teenager, but a distinguished looking soldier. He lost a lot of weight. He dropped about three pants' sizes and was wearing his tall, lanky dad's pants. His shirt was tucked in without a single trace of wrinkles anywhere. His shoes were polished. His hair was buzzed and not one hair was longer than the others. His posture was different. He didn't slack but stood erect. An overwhelming sense of pride seemed to exude from him. He told us that he had

[25] Charles Spurgeon, *Devotional Classics of C. H. Spurgeon* (Mt. Juliet, TN: Sovereign Grace Publishers, 2000), 303.

woken up at four o'clock that morning to sweep off his driveway. The dirt on his driveway apparently caused his sleep to be interrupted. He was now a military man living in a civilian world.

God does more than clone us; He makes us a new creation!

He was no longer a clown, but a clone. He was exactly what the military wanted him to be. A few years later, after he had served his time in the Marines, he went back to being the same goofy guy I knew in high school.

God does more than clone us; He makes us a new creation!

Let me share a few secrets of being a good soldier of Christ. A good soldier knows what he is signing up for. Luke 14:28 says, "For which of you, intending to build a tower, does not sit down first and count the cost, whether he has enough to finish it…?" Most people enlist into God's army not knowing what to expect. It is this lack of knowledge that causes them to sometimes go AWOL. They are not able to juggle their civilian life with their new life.

Verse 4 of 2 Timothy 2 says, "To please the recruiter, no one gets entangled in the concerns of everyday life." It takes a while for an earthly soldier to acclimate to his environment. He misses his home, family, friends, the food he used to eat, and the time he used to have all for himself. It isn't easy for him, but eventually he adjusts to this new home; and when he goes back to his old home, he can't help but be what the military designed him to be.

Sometimes new Christians are lost, trying to find where they fit in. Everything that they know has been interrupted. This is why we need good discipleship programs that create an element of safety, while at the same time offer an environment to grow in the Lord. New Christians need to be plunged into this atmosphere, being branded by the fire of God, and trained to handle the Word of God. This will keep them from being a mile wide and an inch deep.

The church then begins to be their city of refuge, a safe harbor. I find the more people disconnect from the local church, the more they fall victim to retreating back to their old lifestyles and habits. The church gets bad-mouthed more than any other institution in the world, but the truth is, it is still a mighty force on this earth.

A good soldier is subject to his authorities. If I enlist, or sign on the dotted line, I'm agreeing that I belong to that branch of the military. Their motto becomes my motto; their lifestyle becomes my lifestyle. I begin to follow their codes, regulations, and standards. I am no longer free to act as a civilian. I sleep when they want me to, shower when they want me to, and speak when they want me to. In short, I give up my rights to take on their cause.

Hebrews 13:17 says, "Obey those who rule over you, and be submissive, for they watch out for your souls, as those who must give account. Let them do so with joy and not with grief, for that would be unprofitable for you." Leaders are not here to enforce burdensome laws. The Pharisees inflicted the people with strict laws that had nothing to do with God's Torah. Jesus rebuked them with this statement; "They bind heavy burdens, and lay them on men's shoulders; but they themselves will not move them with one of their fingers" (Matthew 23:4).

As your shepherd, the pastor watches over your souls. He is there to protect you and help ensure that you are guided safely on the course that God has put you on. We need to make sure that we submit to the leadership of our pastors so that their job can be carried out with joy instead of grief. I don't want to be one who gives my pastor gray hair, or worse yet, cause his hair to fall out.

A good soldier wears the insignia of his military proudly. Not only does the soldier sign on the dotted line to enlist, but the military itself also puts their mark on him. I'm able to distinguish the different branches of the military by inspecting the uniforms that the soldiers wear. I can tell a Navy officer from an Army Ranger simply by looking at their outfits.

Revelation 3:12 says, "He who overcomes, I will make him a pillar in the temple of My God, and he shall go out no more. I will write on him the name of My God and the name of the city of My God, the New Jerusalem, which comes down out of heaven from My God. And I will write on him My new name."

Our identity is eternally etched into our new man. As we are in Christ as a new creation He marks us by writing His name on us. He wants to make it evident to us whose we are. If we are His then we have been given an inheritance that is beyond measure. We have been given the assurance of salvation and the promise that we can "boldly approach the throne room of grace and find help in the time of need" (Hebrews 4:16).

Our identity is eternally etched into our new man.

Unfortunately some wars have been fought and won by dishonest men who have put on the opposing military's uniform. We need to watch out because our enemy comes as a "wolf in sheep's clothing" and also as an "angel of light." There are so many religions that offer a "spiritual experience" but that are not based on sound, biblical truth. We need to be cautious as to what we involve ourselves with and whom we involve ourselves with. Ground yourself in His Word, get in a Bible-believing church, and hold fast to your God-given convictions. In Acts 2:42 it says, "And they devoted themselves to the apostles' teaching, to fellowship, to the breaking of bread, and to prayers."

Sign on the Dotted Line

The legal definition of signed is accept, accredit, acknowledge, agree to, approve, authenticate, authorize, autograph, certify, confirm, covenant, enter into a contract, indorse, and initial.[26] All this is what God does when we sign up for His service. In 2 Timothy chapter two, the Bible refers to us as good soldiers of Christ. Before we can be a soldier we must first show our commitment by enlisting. A person can talk about being a soldier all they want, but until they enlist they are still just a civilian.

Not only does God put His signature on us, but He also seals what He has done, through His Spirit. Ephesians 1:13-14 says, "In Him you also trusted, after you heard the word of truth, the gospel of your salvation; in whom also, having believed, you were sealed with the Holy Spirit of promise, who is the guarantee of our inheritance until the redemption of the purchased possession, to the praise of His glory."

Sealed

This word sealed comes from the Greek word *sphragizo,* which means to stamp (with a signet or private mark) for security or preservation; to keep secret, to attest, seal up.

Let's now turn our focus to the work of the Holy Spirit in our lives. I want to focus on John 14:16-18. John 14:16-18 verse 16 says, "And I will pray the Father, and He will give you another Helper, that He may abide with you forever." I want to look at three things from this Scripture.

1. Jesus is preparing His disciples for His departure. I believe Jesus is trying to awake in them urgency for the hour they are living in. There needs to be a certain level of holy discontentment in our walk with the Lord. Until we see Him face-to-face and know Him as we are fully known, we should be constantly conscious of the reality of our need for more of Him. Jesus was not looking to bring comfort to His disciples, but to prepare them to be steadfast in the face of persecution. Great grace flows

[26] Definition from legal-dictionary.thefreedictionary.com.

out of having a sense of urgency to reach the unreached. No longer was He going to be there to take care of every situation that they got themselves into. No longer was He going to be there to answer all of their questions. He was trying to produce in them maturity. It was time for them to stop drinking the milk and learn how to eat the meat. It was time for them to grow up.

2. Jesus and the Father were making preparations for His departure. God is always prepared. Since He is always prepared, He is never caught off guard. God has a plan. He knows exactly what He wants to do in your life. He knows exactly what He has knit you together for.

3. He was sending the Holy Spirit to be with us forever. There is never going to be a time when the Holy Spirit has to depart from us. This had to be a comforting thought considering Jesus' departure was at hand. The Holy Spirit is the Counselor, but His Greek name is *parakletos*, which means an intercessor, consoler, advocate, comforter. Do any of these names sound familiar?

Jesus is seated at the right hand of the Father forever making intercession for us. He is the One who had been consoling the disciples. He is the One who is our Advocate with the Father, and He is the Prince of Peace that brings us comfort. So what is Jesus saying? He is saying, "I am sending you someone who is exactly like Me, but is a Spirit who could be everywhere, with every believer, all at once."

If they needed help, they could now call on the Holy Spirit. If they had a question that needed answered, they could now just ask the Holy Spirit. They did not have to worry about waiting in line to get what they needed from Jesus. They did not have to fight the crowds or each other to get His attention. This is truly remarkable!

Verse 17 of John 14 says, "the Spirit of truth, whom the world cannot receive, because it neither sees Him nor knows

Him; but you know Him, for He dwells with you and will be in you." Let's break this up.

He is the Spirit of truth. He is the only truth. You can trust what He says. In verse 26 of John 14, Jesus told the disciples that the Holy Spirit would teach them all things and remind them of everything He had told them.

The world was unable to receive Him because it didn't even see Him or know Him. All the world knows is the spirit of antichrist. Their thought life, reasoning, and intellect leave no room for God. If you don't believe this is true just go to the universities, or look at the curriculum your child is being taught in school. One glance and you will be able to tell of what spirit this world is controlled by. If they have been able to pass along their agenda into our school systems, how much more is it important for us to pass our agenda along in school?

The church should be the most influential organization on earth. Through the power of the Holy Spirit we can cause a spiritual revolution to erupt in our school systems, which will shape and mold the way students, are taught for years to come. This comes through the demonstration of the Spirit's power. God's Kingdom is not a matter of talk, but of power.

The world might not know Him, but we do. As we remain in Him, He remains in us. He anoints, and will give us *dunamis* power. He is with us and in us.

I remember getting a chance to pray with my aunt one evening during a difficult time in her life. As we prayed and encouraged her, the presence of the Lord began to minister to her in ways that only He can. She ended up calling a lot of her family over that night and shared with them about what God had done for her. God always knows exactly what people need, and when they need it.

Verse 18 of John 14 says, "I will not leave you as orphans; I will come to you." The Holy Spirit was also sent to us as a reminder that Jesus was coming back for us. Ephesians 1:14 says, "...who is the guarantee of our inheritance until the redemption of the purchased possession, to the praise of His glory."

Power for All Generations

Here is the good news for us today. The Holy Spirit is still the same Holy Spirit that He was on the day of Pentecost. He is the same Holy Spirit that was with the disciples in the book of Acts. He hasn't changed, but we have.

In Acts 1:8 Jesus said, "We shall receive power after the Holy Spirit has come upon us, and we shall be witnesses" (paraphrased). If you have been baptized in the Spirit you don't need another baptism. The baptism you received was good enough.

In Acts 2:4 the 120 were filled with the Holy Ghost and spoke in tongues as the Spirit gave them utterance. Then Peter stood up and preached, seeing three thousand souls added to the church that day. In Acts 4:31 we read, "When they had prayed, the place where they were assembled was shaken, and they were all filled with the Holy Spirit and began to speak God's message with boldness." In both instances they spoke the Word of God boldly to those who were around.

The Spirit was given to comfort us. He gives us revelation about who Jesus is for the purpose of revealing the heart of God to us and empowering us for acts of service. He is here to make His ministers a flame of fire! You might ask, "How do I receive the Holy Spirit?" Galatians 3:14 says, "That the blessing of Abraham might come upon the Gentiles in Christ Jesus, that we might receive the promise of the Spirit through faith."

You receive Him and the gifts He offers the same way you receive salvation: by faith.

Chapter 9

The Mystery Revealed

"It gives me a deep comforting sense that things seen are temporal and things unseen are eternal."[27]

—Helen Keller

It is part of human nature to be attracted to and intrigued by the mysterious. This is definitely seen in the life of a child. As children, our interest is piqued by the mystery of the unknown. To the child, the unknown has to be exposed, explained, and experienced. To them the adventure of a lifetime could be right around the corner; streams become rivers, trees become forests, and hills become mountains to conquer. As years go by we can lose that sense of adventure. Nothing is a mystery to us anymore, because in our minds we have already experienced it all.

An excerpt from Oswald Chambers, in *My Utmost for His Highest*:

> Our natural inclination is to be so precise—trying always to forecast accurately what will happen next—that we look upon uncertainty as a bad thing. We think

[27] Helen Keller quote taken from http://www.thinkexist.com.

that we must reach some predetermined goal, but that is not the nature of the spiritual life. The nature of the spiritual life is that we are certain in our uncertainty. Consequently, we do not put down roots. Our common sense says, "Well, what if I were in that circumstance?" We cannot presume to see ourselves in any circumstance in which we have never been. Certainty is the mark of the commonsense life—gracious uncertainty is the mark of the spiritual life. To be certain of God means that we are uncertain in all our ways, not knowing what tomorrow may bring. This is generally expressed with a sigh of sadness, but it should be an expression of breathless expectation. We are uncertain of the next step, but we are certain of God. As soon as we abandon ourselves to God and do the task He has placed closest to us, He begins to fill our lives with surprises.

When we become simply a promoter or a defender of a particular belief, something within us dies. That is not believing God—it is only believing our belief about Him. Jesus said, "…unless you…become as little children…" (Matthew 18:3). The spiritual life is the life of a child. We are not uncertain of God, just uncertain of what He is going to do next. If our certainty is only in our beliefs, we develop a sense of self-righteousness, become overly critical, and are limited by the view that our beliefs are complete and settled. But when we have the right relationship with God, life is full of spontaneous, joyful uncertainty and expectancy. Jesus said, "…believe also in Me" (John 14:1), not, "Believe certain things about Me". Leave everything to Him and it will be gloriously and graciously uncertain how He will come in—but you can be certain that He will come. Remain faithful to Him. [28]

---

[28] Oswald Chambers, *My Utmost for His Highest,* "Gracious Uncertainty" (Uhrichsville, OH: Barbour Publishing, 1924), April 29.

The very nature and person of God is a mystery. In the wilderness He led the children of Israel in a cloud by day and fire by night. This same God who dwelt in thick darkness and who also wrapped Himself in unapproachable light has now been revealed to us through His Son. Even the way He chooses to do things is a mystery to us; but as Oswald Chambers says in this devotion, "Leave everything to Him and it will be gloriously uncertain how He will come in—but you can be certain He will come." Our unseen, often mysterious God has called us to go on an amazing adventure with Him! He just asks that we walk by faith, not by sight.

Our unseen, often mysterious God has called us to go on an amazing adventure with Him! He just asks that we walk by faith, not by sight.

As Christians, we are called to manifest the mystery of the Gospel. First Corinthians 4:1 says, "Let a man consider us, as servants of Christ and stewards of the mystery of God."

I did not grow up in a Christian home. The only godly influence I had was my grandparents. My grandpa is a pastor of a small Pentecostal church in Illinois. I have a close relationship with my grandparents. It was because of their influence in my life that one night, very reluctantly, I accepted an invitation to attend a revival meeting with them.

The service was strange to me, and I didn't understand why people worshipped God the way they did. The way they dressed was also very old-fashioned. It was mysterious, but at the same time very liberating to see people so expressive in their worship. I must say that from the moment I walked through the back door of this church I felt something deep in my gut that I couldn't quite shake. The passion of the worshippers was only rivaled by the intensity of the speaker.

The evangelist spoke a message out of Ezekiel 37 entitled, "Are you dry bones or live bones?" I was gripped from the very beginning of his message until his closing. As he gave the invitation that night, I rushed forward, dropped to my knees, and spent the next two hours crying out to a God I didn't see, but I could definitely feel! That was the start of an awesome journey with an unseen God who desperately desired to make Himself known to me! As I discover the mystery of this Good News, I am compelled to make Him known to others!

Fishing with Jesus

One of my favorite pastimes is going fishing with my grandpa. When I was younger we would frequent the local ponds hoping to catch a big bass. My grandpa taught me everything he knew about bass fishing. There were many occasions where I would fish all day with him. Sometimes we would fish in ponds and other times out in the lake, on his boat. It seemed as if every time I went fishing with him, no matter how bad the fish were biting, he would always catch something. My uncle, who was also an avid bass angler, would joke about my grandpa being the only person he knew who could use the cheapest worms and still catch fish when no one else could!

Jesus gave us the perfect bait to catch the attention of these land-dwelling fish—Himself!

Jesus is the best fishing partner we could ever hope to have. He always knows where the fish are and what they are biting on. The Bible records a few different fishing stories of Jesus. Unlike some of our fishing stories, His are always true and never embellished. Christ has called us to go on a very special fishing trip with Him. These fish don't live in the water, but in the world.

Jesus gave us the perfect bait to catch the attention of these land-dwelling fish—Himself! He knew that if He was lifted up they would be drawn to Him. Different fish require specific bait. Some go after live bait and others prefer their bait dead. Jesus offered Himself as the perfect sacrifice for our sins. Jesus allowed His blood to be spilled by our hands so that His blood could be applied to our hearts.

Just like fish, people are constantly changing, growing, and adapting to new phases of life. Proverbs 20:5 says, "Counsel in the heart of man is as deep waters, but a man of understanding will draw it out." We are called both to diagnose the problem and to deal with it. In the past the church had been good at pointing out sin, but not very good at offering the remedy for sin.

The remedy for sin is always Jesus. The more in love I am with Him, the less I desire sin. The more in love the church is with Him, the less backbiting, gossip, strife, envy, and pride will dominate our holy union with our heavenly Father.

The Thriving Church

I believe that the church has been going through an amazing shift. God is restoring the bridal affections of this once cold-hearted establishment and ushering in a new era of unbridled intimacy. This newfound intimacy is shifting the modern church as we know it.

Consider this. A recent book on missional house churches showed that the church in China (which is a network of underground churches) sees an average of 30,000 believers baptized every day![29] The church has survived every kind of persecution known to man, but still continues to grow in the face of opposition. In the past hundred years the church has seen its greatest harvest of souls ever! The church is not dying; it's growing and becoming a force that sees nations saved in a day! Before we bash the church, let's consider that we are a part of the church. So, if we are not helping bring the solution, then we are just adding to the problem.

---

[29] J. D. Payne, *Missional House Churches* (Kingstown Broadway, Carlisle, Cumbria: Paternoster, 2008), 143.

Ephesians 3:8-11 says, "To me, who am less than the least of all the saints, this grace was given, that I should preach among the Gentiles the unsearchable riches of Christ, and to make all see what is the fellowship of the mystery, which from the beginning of the ages has been hidden in God who created all things through Jesus Christ; to the intent that now the manifold wisdom of God might be made known by the church to the principalities and powers in the heavenly places, according to the eternal purpose which He accomplished in Christ Jesus our Lord."

Paul made it his mission to make plain to everyone this mystery. It is also our calling to make plain to others what has already been made plain to us: that is Christ and Him crucified. Not only does God give us a platform to preach to people, but He also gives us the angels as our audience. Verse 10 from Ephesians 3 says "His intent was that now, through the church, the manifold wisdom of God should be made known to the rulers and authorities in the heavenly realms."

Second Corinthians 2:14 says, "Now thanks be to God who always leads us in triumph in Christ, and through us diffuses the fragrance of His knowledge in every place." Our worship and obedience is a sweet-smelling fragrance to God. The combination of undivided worship and radical obedience releases His fragrance into our lives. Without His fragrance we are helpless in reaching the lost. Our words will be empty, and every attempt will appear shallow. His aroma on us is His validation of us. If there is no anointing, people will be able to tell. It should be our desire to see a culture infused with the knowledge of God. This culture will never be infused with this knowledge until we are first willing to diffuse this knowledge.

His aroma on us is His validation of us.

Habakkuk 2:14 says, "For the earth will be filled with the knowledge of the Lord's glory, as the waters cover the sea." The knowledge of God is presented through the people of God. In other words, the knowledge of His glory will cover the earth when we cover the earth and share this message of redemption and forgiveness to people.

When we preach the Gospel we are giving creation what it has been waiting for. Romans 8:19-21 says, "For the creation eagerly waits with anticipation for God's sons to be revealed. For the creation was subjected to futility—not willingly, but because of Him who subjected it—in the hope that the creation itself will also be set free from the bondage of corruption into the glorious freedom of God's children" (CSB).

When we preach the Gospel we are giving creation what it has been waiting for.

In Luke 8:10 Jesus says, "...To you it has been given to know the mysteries of the Kingdom of God, but to the rest it is given in parables, that seeing they may not see, and hearing they may not understand." The truth is that some people will not even want to listen, but there will always be honest seekers who are ready to receive the Gospel. That is why we are compelled to preach and share our testimony with others.

Jeremiah said the "Word of God is in me like a fire shut up in my bones, and I am weary from holding it back." All the unholy host of hell should reel under the torrents of an unstoppable spiritual tsunami proceeding from God's holy people. God makes His ministers a flame of fire. It should make us tired trying to hold in what was meant to come out. May we be a new breed of revivalists eager to impart what has been freely given to us!

Listen Up

"He who has an ear, let him hear what the Spirit says to the churches" (Revelation 2:29). This phrase is repeated seven times to the seven churches of Asia mentioned in Revelation. Do you ever get the feeling that God is trying to drive home a very important truth? This is not only a truth that affected these particular churches, but it's also a truth that rings true with all churches down through history. Not only do we need to hear what the Spirit is saying to the church, but the lost also need us to hear, because their salvation is dependent upon how well we hear and then deliver the message that was delivered to us.

Swimmer's ear is something I've dealt with ever since I was a child. I still remember when I was about ten years old; I was taken to the hospital to get plugs put in my ears. This was the first, and only time since, that I've spent the night in the hospital. I thought this condition would pass with time, but it has not. The doctor told me when I was younger that I had very windy ear canals and that it was hard for water to properly drain out of my ear. Strangely enough, this has never deterred me from going swimming without earplugs.

It's human nature to overlook certain conditions that are not causing pain and discomfort. It is when these conditions escalate that we scramble to find relief. Recently I've been dealing with an ear infection. It has been very uncomfortable. Due to the excess wax buildup that a cotton swab cannot get to, it has caused bacteria to get in my ear and caused it to swell shut. The only way to get the wax out is to get my ears flushed. I never knew how much I enjoyed hearing out of that ear until this happened and I could barely hear!

As the church we have been given the unique opportunity of hearing what God is speaking. Sometimes we forget how much of a privilege this is. We come down with our own case of spiritual swimmer's ear. We long to hear from God and question why He does not speak. We blame Him for being distant and out of touch. We must never point the finger at God and accuse Him of wanting to remain silent. He wants to speak to us. He wants to have relationship with us.

First Peter 2:9 says, "But you are a chosen generation, a royal priesthood, a holy nation, His own special people, that you may proclaim the praises of Him who called you out of darkness into His marvelous light." This word chosen can also mean favorite in the original Greek. Did you know that you are God's favorite? God cherishes every moment with you. He longs to make Himself known to you. So, why is it that He seems so silent at times, especially those times you feel you need Him the most? Hopefully I can help you find the answer to this question.

God's native language is not English. Isaiah 55:9 says, "For as the heavens are higher than the earth, so are my ways higher than your ways, and my thoughts than your thoughts." How is it that we can hear from God? In verse 11 of this chapter it tells us, "So shall my word be that goeth forth out of My mouth: it shall not return unto me void, but it shall accomplish that which I please, and it shall prosper in the thing whereto I sent it" (Isaiah 55:11, KJV). He looks over His Word to perform it.

If we open up our hearts to God, He opens up His Word to us.

If we open up our hearts to God, He opens up His Word to us. He causes us to hear what we couldn't hear before. Suddenly the Holy Spirit takes what seems to be encrypted and supernaturally decodes it.

We don't hear because we are scared of what He might say, or maybe we have something we are trying to hide. We could call this selective hearing. Once you are married you will understand this phrase a little better! Isaiah 59:2 says, "But your iniquities have separated between you and your God, and your sins have hid his face from you, that he will not hear" (KJV).

When I was younger I was told by my grandpa not to climb on the back of his van. He had already given me a warning. The next time I was going to get a whooping, and you don't want a whooping from a man that is 6 foot 2 inches tall and weighs 260 pounds! As a child this fact did not register in my mind. I remember going against his word and climbing up the van ladder. He came out of his house and tried to catch me, but with quick footwork I escaped. He ran out of steam and went back

Today, God is offering you a second chance. Will you receive His offer?

inside. So I climbed up the van once again. This time he came out and I wasn't quite as lucky. He caught me. He is a kind man, but I was testing his patience.

Sooner or later our sins will catch up with us. We can never outrun God. Eventually He will catch us. We can either come to Him willingly, or the Bible says, it is "a dreadful thing to fall into the hands of the living God" (Hebrews 10:31).

So what do we do when God calls to us? When Stephen was stoned in Acts 7:57, it says, "Then they cried out with a loud voice, and stopped their ears, and ran upon him with one accord" (KJV). They couldn't stand to hear the words that were coming out of his mouth. The words cut to the bone and caused conviction. They knew what he was saying was true. They had a choice. Do we give our life to God, or do we choose to stop our ears and pretend Stephen is to blame?

They made their choice, but one man out of that group, Saul, had an awesome encounter with God. He was given a second chance. Paul could have said, "I'm not changing my life for anybody." Thankfully he made the right choice. He was saved and became the greatest missionary in the Bible. He spread the Gospel to most of the known world at that time. Today, God is offering you a second chance. Will you receive His offer?

Chapter 10

Lifeless Staffs, Lapsed Methods, and the Living Word

There is a stench in the nostrils of God called pride. It is the oldest known sin (originating with Satan). It has been the cause of the ruination of every empire that has ever existed. You would think that something so vile couldn't exist in something as holy as the church, but the truth is, it does. The competitive spirit of the world's system has bled over into the fabric of the church. Now we compete with each other instead of compelling each other onto good works.

Each church tries desperately to win the attention of people so they can add higher numbers to their roster. They will even go as far as putting the other church down to make themselves look better, pointing out where they are right and others are wrong. Allow me to clarify what I mean. I understand that there are glaring theological differences in the way many people interpret Scripture. Since judgment begins in the house of God, we must boldly guard the absolute essentials of our faith. We cannot allow bad doctrine and poor exegesis to run roughshod over the foundational teachings of Scripture.

Unfortunately, division is oftentimes more prevalent in the human traditions and cultural influences of church function. Did Christ die for an undivided church? Is He coming back for only one part of His bride? As Paul said, "Is Christ divided?" No; He has made us one "body" that receives its direction from the head (Christ).

One major area of division centers on evangelism. What is the right way to evangelize? Different ministries boastfully declare that theirs is the only right method for true biblical evangelism. They claim that Jesus had one specific way of reaching people. This couldn't be any farther from the truth.

In actuality, Jesus used multiple outlets to effectively spread the Gospel of the Kingdom. The methods Jesus used were all done out of relationship to His Father. He said, "I can only do what I see My Father doing." We will do well to note this principle in our own personal outreach ministries.

If we have seen limited results in an area, we assume that God is not working that way anymore.

God is a creative God. He does not have to do the same thing the same way He has always done it. You might say, "Well, that sounds unscriptural, because the Bible says that He is the same yesterday, today, and forever." I don't disagree with that Scripture. However, I do disagree with how some interpret that Scripture.

We sometimes foolishly put God in a little box. Usually that box is built upon the premise of our own experiences. If we have seen limited results in an area, we assume that God is not working that way anymore. Maybe we don't see a particular method used in Scripture. I have a friend who has an evangelistic ministry that has a huge focus on reaching people through creative means such as dance, painting, and poems. I never read about Jesus using these methods in the Bible, so is my friend flirting with heresy? Absolutely not! Don't be quick to judge someone else's ministry. God may be using something that seems foolish to you to cofound the wise.

Lifeless Staffs

Allow me to illustrate a couple of examples in the Bible of God placing a somewhat foolish tool in the hands of ordinary men. The two men are Moses and Elisha, and God's tool of choice was a staff.

We all know the story of how God used Moses' staff to help bring deliverance to the children of Israel, but have you heard about Elisha's lifeless staff? Let's look at an example of this in 2 Kings 4:1-37 (ESV);

> **Elisha and the Widow's Oil**
>
> [1] Now the wife of one of the sons of the prophets cried
> to Elisha, "Your servant my husband is dead, and you
> know that your servant feared the Lord, but the cred-
> itor has come to take my two children to be his slaves."
> [2] And Elisha said to her, "What shall I do for you? Tell
> me; what have you in the house?" And she said, "Your
> servant has nothing in the house except a jar of oil."
> [3] Then he said, "Go outside, borrow vessels from all
> your neighbors, empty vessels and not too few. [4] Then
> go in and shut the door behind yourself and your sons
> and pour into all these vessels. And when one is full,
> set it aside." [5] So she went from him and shut the door
> behind herself and her sons. And as she poured they
> brought the vessels to her. [6] When the vessels were full,
> she said to her son, "Bring me another vessel." And he
> said to her, "There is not another." Then the oil stopped
> flowing. [7] She came and told the man of God, and he
> said, "Go, sell the oil and pay your debts, and you and
> your sons can live on the rest."

Elisha and the Shunammite Woman

8 One day Elisha went on to Shunem, where a wealthy woman lived, who urged him to eat some food. So whenever he passed that way, he would turn in there to eat food. 9 And she said to her husband, "Behold now, I know that this is a holy man of God who is continually passing our way. 10 Let us make a small room on the roof with walls and put there for him a bed, a table, a chair, and a lamp, so that whenever he comes to us, he can go in there."

11 One day he came there, and he turned into the chamber and rested there. 12 And he said to Gehazi his servant, "Call this Shunammite." When he had called her, she stood before him. 13 And he said to him, "Say now to her, 'See, you have taken all this trouble for us; what is to be done for you? Would you have a word spoken on your behalf to the king or to the commander of the army?'" She answered, "I dwell among my own people." 14 And he said, "What then is to be done for her?" Gehazi answered, "Well, she has no son, and her husband is old." 15 He said, "Call her." And when he had called her, she stood in the doorway. 16 And he said, "At this season, about this time next year, you shall embrace a son." And she said, "No, my lord, O man of God; do not lie to your servant." 17 But the woman conceived, and she bore a son about that time the following spring, as Elisha had said to her.

Elisha Raises the Shunammite's Son

18 When the child had grown, he went out one day to his father among the reapers. 19 And he said to his father, "Oh, my head, my head!" The father said to his servant, "Carry him to his mother." 20 And when he had lifted him and brought him to his mother, the child sat on her lap till noon, and then he died. 21 And she went up and laid him on the bed of the man of God and shut the

door behind him and went out. [22] Then she called to her husband and said, "Send me one of the servants and one of the donkeys, that I may quickly go to the man of God and come back again." [23] And he said, "Why will you go to him today? It is neither new moon nor Sabbath." She said, "All is well." [24] Then she saddled the donkey, and she said to her servant, "Urge the animal on; do not slacken the pace for me unless I tell you." [25] So she set out and came to the man of God at Mount Carmel.

When the man of God saw her coming, he said to Gehazi his servant, "Look, there is the Shunammite. [26] Run at once to meet her and say to her, 'Is all well with you? Is all well with your husband? Is all well with the child?'" And she answered, "All is well." [27] And when she came to the mountain to the man of God, she caught hold of his feet. And Gehazi came to push her away. But the man of God said, "Leave her alone, for she is in bitter distress, and the Lord has hidden it from me and has not told me." [28] Then she said, "Did I ask my lord for a son? Did I not say, 'Do not deceive me?'" [29] He said to Gehazi, "Tie up your garment and take my staff in your hand and go. If you meet anyone, do not greet him, and if anyone greets you, do not reply. And lay my staff on the face of the child." [30] Then the mother of the child said, "As the Lord lives and as you yourself live, I will not leave you." So he arose and followed her. [31] Gehazi went on ahead and laid the staff on the face of the child, but there was no sound or sign of life. Therefore he returned to meet him and told him, "The child has not awakened."

[32] When Elisha came into the house, he saw the child lying dead on his bed. [33] So he went in and shut the door behind the two of them and prayed to the Lord. [34] Then he went up and lay on the child, putting his mouth on his mouth, his eyes on his eyes, and his hands on his hands. And as he stretched himself upon him, the

> flesh of the child became warm. 35 Then he got up again
> and walked once back and forth in the house, and went
> up and stretched himself upon him. The child sneezed
> seven times, and the child opened his eyes. 36 Then he
> summoned Gehazi and said, "Call this Shunammite." So
> he called her. And when she came to him, he said, "Pick
> up your son." 37 She came and fell at his feet, bowing to
> the ground. Then she picked up her son and went out.

Did you notice anything strange about Elisha's staff? His idea of using the staff to bring the boy back to life was powerless. It wasn't until Elisha personally went to the grieving mother's house and laid his own body over her child that the boy was miraculously brought back to life. When was the last time the church got this close to a generation? Maybe it's time to go where people are hurting the most so we can introduce them to our "Great Physician."

He is searching for a flesh-and-blood believer who will not be afraid to stretch his body out over a lifeless generation.

Does God have the ability to use a staff to perform miracles? Of course He does. God is all-powerful! He can use whatever means He wants to bring about His will on earth. Just because He used the staff once doesn't mean that will be His preferred method forever. He needs someone with an open heart and attentive ear to hear what He is saying at any specific moment. God is not looking for a robot that is programmed to do whatever He says. He is searching for a flesh-and-blood believer who will not be afraid to stretch his body out over a lifeless generation.

Elisha was able to follow the leading of the Spirit in a very crucial moment. When pressures come, God wants us to trust Him all the more to give us the right methods. I've found that the greatest breakthroughs oftentimes come when we least expect it. When your back is against the wall, will you trust God?

The Living Word

God anoints His Word and causes it not to return to Him void. He is not obligated to anoint our methods and programs, but He has bound Himself to His Word. Read His Word aloud so faith will be rooted in your heart. When Jesus was tempted in the wilderness He told Satan in Matthew 4:4, "Man shall not live by bread alone, but by every word that proceedeth out of the mouth of God" (KJV). Here, the word proceed is in the present tense. This Scripture proves that God is currently speaking. It is not enough just to have a word from God yesterday. We must hear and obey what He is saying today. I think this is why so many people get stuck in a spiritual rut. What is God speaking to you today? Find out, and then act on it. That is called faith.

God's soft-spoken words to our heart give us understanding of His written Word.

We can never say that God is not speaking. He has been speaking to us from the time He asked Adam, "Where are you?" until the present age of the church. It is imperative that we hear His *rhema* word for our life. God's soft-spoken words to our heart give us understanding of His written Word. He is searching for both our availability and our vulnerability.

God Is in the Details

Listed below are some practical pointers to consider when engaging others with the message of Jesus:

1. **We must pray.** Prayer opens doors that no amount of preaching could ever open. The disciples asked Jesus to teach them to pray. They didn't ask Jesus to give them a book of His best sermons. It was obvious to them that everything Jesus did was birthed out of prayer.

2. **Always remember to show love.** Love should be the oil we dip our every word in. If people don't see and hear

love in your voice, they will immediately turn a deaf ear to you. I think we will be judged more strictly by God concerning how much love we showed to people than in reference to any other gift. God is love. Mike Bickel, founder of the International House of Prayer, said, "It takes God to love God."[30] Robert Murray McCheyene said, "The love of Christ is like the blue sky, into which you may see clearly, but the real vastness of which you cannot measure."[31]

3. **We must always keep in mind that man has a dilemma. He was born into sin.** No matter how good the person may sound, if he or she does not have a living relationship with Jesus they are doomed to experience the wrath of God. God loves them, but He is also just. Jesus experienced the wrath of man, but unrepentant men will come under the wrath of God. People need to know the gravity of rejecting Jesus.

4. **God gave a solution to man's dilemma.** "He made Him who knew no sin to be sin for us, that we might become the righteousness of God" (2 Corinthians 5:21). We can have right standing with God only through Jesus.

5. **Using the law is a good way to show people they are in sin.** The Ten Commandments were given to us for a reason. They help shed light on people's sin. They show us God's moral guideline. Some people have hardened themselves to God and need to be confronted with their sin and denial head on. The Ten Commandments were first given to Moses as a moral compass for the people of Israel. They had just come out of the Egyptian culture with its worship of false gods and immoral

---

[30] Mike Bickle, excerpt from the message, "Loving God: The First Commandment Restored to First Place," April 8, 2010.

[31] Robert Murray McCheyene, *The Works of the Late Rev. Robert Murray McCheyne* (New York: R. Carter, not in copyright), 435.

living. They were imprisoned in Egypt for nearly four hundred years. God had to reset their way of thinking. The Ten Commandments were one tool He used to give a clear example of what He required from them. In our American judicial system, the Ten Commandments have been a concrete way to help try, and convict criminals. It's only in recent years that God's laws have come under severe attacks by the ACLU and other organizations. The more the Commandments are attacked, the more media exposure they receive. What the enemy meant for bad, God is turning around for good. Most people have a general knowledge of the Ten Commandments. This is why it is a useful tool in reaching the lost. You get to start at a level people can understand. Even people who cannot quote John 3:16 know that murder and stealing is wrong. As with any other method there are times when this is what God wants to use and times when it is not.

6. **Be sensitive to the Holy Spirit.** If we do not allow the Holy Spirit to lead us, we could end up being harsh at a time when we are supposed to be soft, or we could be too easygoing at a time when we should be bold. Do not be deafened by the sound of your own voice. Some believers love to hear their own voice. We must remember that it is the Spirit of God who "convicts the world of sin, righteousness, and judgment." It is His Spirit that draws all men to Christ, and it is His Sprit that brings to our remembrance all things concerning Jesus. We must have a dependence on God to give us the right words at the right time. The Holy Spirit gives us gifts as He wills. He may show you something personal about someone's life and then lead you to share it with them. I've had a few different encounters with people where the Holy Spirit gave me a direct word for them, resulting in that person receiving salvation.

7. **Use your testimony.** This is a powerful way to convey what God is doing in the modern world. It shows unbelievers that God is actively changing lives. A testimony is the product of the Gospel in action. It is also a constant reminder to the enemy that Jesus is winning. Revelation 12:11 says, "We overcome him by the blood of the Lamb and the word of our testimony" (paraphrased). Testimonies are a modern-day account of God's dealings in the affairs of men. It's easy for people to argue theology with us; it's easy for people to flaunt their opinions; but it is not easy for them to debunk your own experience with Jesus. Your testimony helps tear down their false imaginations about an unloving, unjust God. It shows people that if God is willing to bless an ordinary person like you, then He can bless them as well. It is also a way of releasing the spirit of prophesy into your conversation. Revelation 19:10 tells us, "… the testimony of Jesus is the spirit of prophecy."
8. **Be bold and confident in the Lord.** Speak with boldness and excitement in your voice as you're sharing your faith. Communication is just as much how you say something as what you say. There are few things more frustrating than when a Christian gives an intimidated, stale account of their salvation. The early church burned with a radical message of hope. So should we. In 2 Timothy 1:7 it says, "God did not give you a spirit of fear, but of love, power, and a sound mind" (paraphrased). We should anticipate that the Lord is going to do great things.
9. **See if there is anybody sick in body that you can pray for.** It is hard to deny the fact that much of Jesus' ministry was about bringing healing to the broken, hurting, and sick people of the world. We must be about that same business. He told His disciples in Matthew 10:7-8, "As you go, preach, saying, 'The Kingdom

of God is at hand.' Heal the sick, cleanse the lepers, and raise the dead...." Offer to pray with them about their needs. Most people will accept prayer. Prayer is very important because every time you pray you invite God's presence into that situation. Your prayers position people to receive healing.

10. **Listen to what the other person has to say.** Don't be quick to insert your opinion, especially when they are talking. Their breakthrough could come as a result of their own statements. Jesus oftentimes used the words of His hearers to drive home valuable spiritual lessons. The Samaritan woman at the well is a prime example. Who would have ever thought that a conversation about well water could have led to an entire village believing on Jesus?

11. **Don't give an answer to a question you don't know.** Some people will ask you questions just to trip you up. Don't make up the answers. Get back to them later if you have to.

12. **Make sure to keep them on track with the Gospel.** Paul said in Romans 1:16, "For I am not ashamed of the gospel of Christ: for it is the power of God unto salvation to every one that believeth; to the Jew first, and also to the Greek" (KJV). The enemy wants to distract us from preaching the Good News because he understands the potential and power of its message.

13. **Plug new believers into a good church.** We must make disciples. If people are not properly discipled, then discouragement can set in and they will become easy prey for the enemy. Think about the disciples. After Jesus died on the cross they went back fishing. If they walked with Jesus and still couldn't commit to His mission during the three days of His absence, what makes us think infant Christians would do any better?

We must take ownership of our part in the Great Commission. We must be torchbearers for our generation. We must not let our fire go out. God is depending on us to make an eternal difference in the lives of those around us.

Chapter 11

Lifesaver

William Booth said, "While women weep, as they do now, I'll fight; while children go hungry, as they do now I'll fight; while men go to prison, in and out, in and out, as they do now, I'll fight; while there is a drunkard left, while there is a poor lost girl upon the streets, while there remains one dark soul without the light of God, I'll fight, I'll fight to the very end!"[32]

A lot of Christians' lives are shrouded in unbelief, worry and anxiety, fearfulness and failure, are paralyzed by their past, and doubting their future. They have been manipulated by the ones they love the most and have felt overlooked by the church. Everything piles up over time until people reach a breaking point.

Two things can happen at this point. They leave the church and become bitter, or they become institutionalized. If they leave, they inevitably take other people with them. Bitterness is like poison to a church. Many churches have fallen victim to some who feel victimized themselves. If bitter people remain

---

[32] An excerpt from William Booth's final speech on May 9, 1912, at the Royal Albert Hall in London to a packed crowd of seven thousand Salvationists. "William Booth," Wikiquote, http://en.wikiquote.org/wiki/William_Booth.

offended and do not leave the church, they can become a stumbling block for others; or they become institutionalized, and lose their passion for God and people. They stop thinking about ways to benefit the church and become very inward. Of course their spiritual bankruptcy is not only a product of their own choices, but it is also a mark on the church.

We must find these sinking people! Some are at the point of going under for the last time!

We must find these sinking people! Some are at the point of going under for the last time! It is not just the pastor's job to reach out to these people. It amazes me how much pressure we put on a single man. We expect him to do things we do not do, and sometimes we expect him to come into our sphere of influence and reach the people we have not been willing to reach ourselves.

You know something is terribly wrong when a man not even related to your family has a greater interest in their salvation than you do. The pastor can help equip us to reach them and even pray in agreement with us on their behalf, but it is our responsibility to present Jesus to them.

Dreamers and Doers

In life there are dreamers and doers. We need them both. They are in a divine cooperation with each other. They keep each other alive. The dreamer without the doer is living a pipe dream. The doer without the dreamer sometimes misses the big picture, or loses the childlike sense of awe and faith that is needed to carry out a God-sized mission.

America was built by dreamers who envisioned a better world to live in. It was also built by the blood, sweat, and tears of hard workers. The cross was the climax of the blood, sweat, and tears of Jesus, but it was "for the joy set before Him that He endured the cross." His vision of "sitting down at the right hand of God" and bringing many sinners to righteousness pushed Him past the pain He endured by the hands of man.

You can only tread water for so long until you start to sink. … God specializes in saving sinking people!

Dreams help carry us through the rough patches of life. They reveal the light at the end of the tunnel. We must help people begin to dream again! When a person stops dreaming, they start drowning. The Bible puts it this way, "Where there is no vision, the people perish" (Proverbs 29:18, KJV). You can only tread water for so long until you start to sink.

We usually cling to the strong and let the weak drown, but David said in Psalm 40:2, "God lifted me up out of a deep pit, …and set my feet on a firm foundation." God specializes in saving sinking people!

Matthew 14:22-31 (ESV):

22 Immediately he made the disciples get into the boat
and go before him to the other side, while he dismissed
the crowds. 23 And after he had dismissed the crowds,
he went up on the mountain by himself to pray. When
evening came, he was there alone, 24 but the boat by this
time was a long way from the land, beaten by the waves,
for the wind was against them. 25 And in the fourth
watch of the night he came to them, walking on the sea.
26 But when the disciples saw him walking on the sea,
they were terrified, and said, "It is a ghost!" and they
cried out in fear. 27 But immediately Jesus spoke to them,
saying, "Take heart; it is I. Do not be afraid."

28 And Peter answered him, "Lord, if it is you, command
me to come to you on the water." 29 He said, "Come."
So Peter got out of the boat and walked on the water
and came to Jesus. 30 But when he saw the wind, he was
afraid, and beginning to sink he cried out, "Lord, save

> me." [31] Jesus immediately reached out his hand and took hold of him, saying to him, "O you of little faith, why did you doubt?"

Notice God did not save Peter when he began to sink. He saved him when Peter called out, "Lord, save me!" We have all been infused with an instinctual knowledge to cry out for help when we are in peril. Thank God for this knowledge!

Isaiah 55:6 says, "Seek the Lord while He may be found and call on Him when He is near." Don't wait until you have sunk to the bottom before you cry out to Him. While Peter was close to Jesus on the water he cried out to Him. Jesus' response to Peter's sinking was immediate. He didn't hire a search party to come find Peter after he had sunk. God will treat your heartfelt cry to Him in your moment of need the same as He did for Peter!

We cry out to whatever we are closest to. If a child gets lost from its mother in the grocery store, they cry out for their mother. Everybody else looks scary to them because the child is attached to its mother.

We inwardly seek comfort from those who are most like us.

We inwardly seek comfort from those who are most like us. It would do me no real good to share my innermost thoughts to a total stranger, but Jesus is not a stranger and doesn't want to be treated like one. He wants to help you. He wants to be there when nobody else is, and He will be there when nobody else is. In that moment it is up to you to recognize His presence.

The world tries to tell us that "it doesn't matter what god you cry out to, just as long as you cry out to something." The same people that curse God and use His name in vain are the very ones who call out to Him when things are going bad. A false god is good enough for them when everything is going smoothly, but when the going gets tough, they are reminded of the only One who has the power to save.

The Bible says in Romans 10:13, "Whoever calls on the name of the Lord will be saved." We can be thankful that Isaiah 59:1 says, "Behold, the Lord's hand is not shortened, that it cannot save; neither his ear heavy, that it cannot hear" (KJV).

I look at it this way. If I go buy a suit coat, I don't get a size 42, because I know that won't fit me. If I go ahead and buy the size that fits me, then I don't have to come back and exchange the smaller coat later. Aren't you glad that God doesn't change on us like we change on Him?

Very Present Help

No matter what you are facing in life, God wants to come to your assistance. I find it very sad and disheartening when I hear of people who try, in their own strength, to fight battles without trusting in the Lord. It's like getting caught in quicksand. Wikipedia says quicksand forms when water saturates an area of loose sand and the sand is agitated. When the water trapped in the sand cannot escape, it creates liquefied soil that cannot support weight.

The devil is good at setting traps for people that appear like blessings. All too often we fall for his cunning craftiness. With little to no hesitation we walk out on ground which appears solid, but then we begin to sink. Satan's schemes resemble quicksand. The more we fight with the "weapons of our warfare," the quicker we sink. It is best to see the snares of the enemy before we get ourselves stuck in them. Ben Franklin said, "An ounce of prevention is worth a pound of cure."

God is described by David as a "very present help in time of need." How many of your friends would you describe as a very present help? Some of our friends are more of a hindrance than a help. Some even distract us from our God-given goals in life. I remember the day I moved away from my hometown to embark on my new journey with God. I was moving to a different state six hours away (I thought that was a long distance). It was a bit

When someone is sinking, we can either be sharks or life preservers.

uncomfortable to move away from all that I had known. The night before I left, one of my best friends reaffirmed my decision to move. He knew that if I were to stay, I would be holding myself back from what I was designed to do.

Peter took courage in the fact that Jesus permitted him to walk out on the water with Him. All it took was one simple word, "Come," and Peter left the confines of a comfortable boat to walk on a tempestuous sea. Sometimes all it takes is one person giving us the encouragement we need to take that initial step.

Sharks and Life Preservers

When someone is sinking, we can either be sharks or life preservers.

In World War II there was a ship called the *USS Indianapolis* that was struck by a torpedo fired from a Japanese submarine. When the ship was torpedoed, there were 1,197 sailors and marines inside. Of those men, only 900 survived, only to have to stay in the water for five days until rescuers came and saved them. By the time the rescuers got there, only 317 men were left alive. The wounds that some of the men sustained drew sharks from miles around and the sharks slowly began to pick the wounded soldiers off. They didn't usually attack a large cluster of them. When some of the men began to drink the salty ocean water, they would die quicker of dehydration and the other soldiers would push the dead bodies away so that the sharks would attack the dead soldiers and not the live ones.[33]

---

[33] "The Story," U.S.S. Indianapolis, http://www.ussindianapolis.org/story.htm.

Unfortunately some people in the church can be like these sharks. The weak ones get picked on and gossiped about when these are the very ones we should be helping the most.

James 5:19-20 says, “My brothers, if anyone among you wanders from the truth and someone brings him back, let him know that whoever brings back a sinner from his wandering will save his soul from death and will cover a multitude of sins.”

Galatians 6:1 says, “Brothers, if anyone is caught in any transgression, you who are spiritual should restore him in a spirit of gentleness. Keep watch on yourself, lest you too be tempted.”

Will You Be a Shark or a Life Preserver?

I remember a story my friend told me about going hogging with his youth pastor. Hogging is fishing in lakes or rivers using only your bare hands to catch fish. My friend’s youth pastor had a huge load of fish on a stringer. He had to swim across a deep part of the lake, fully clothed, with about fifty pounds of fish on his back. He couldn’t swim very well in the first place. As he struggled to make it across a large section of the lake he began to sink. My friend turned around just in time to see his youth pastor go under the water. So he swam back out to meet him, dove underneath his feet, and literally became his platform to push off of and get to shore. In doing this my friend almost drowned in the process.

When was the last time you were someone’s platform? When was the last time you were someone’s life preserver? Nobody wants to be a doormat, but it is our privilege, like David declared, to “be a doorkeeper in the house of our God.” There is no greater honor than to be stationed at the doorway to heaven, ushering men and women into His Kingdom!

When was the last time you were someone’s platform? When was the last time you were someone’s life preserver?

If we are not careful we can fall into the trap of bypassing one person just to get to a crowd. We must not allow the lure of the masses to sway us from reaching the individual. Many times Jesus ministered to just one person while whole multitudes of people were left waiting to hear from Him.

Man's desire to have a large fan base can be a detriment to his character and a hindrance to his ministry.

Megachurches and bigger crowds are not the problem. Jesus also had large gatherings of people follow Him and listen to His teachings. However, Jesus walked in complete humility. He did not neglect the one for the attention of many. Man's desire to have a large fan base can be a detriment to his character and a hindrance to his ministry. If we lower the standard of the Word of God enough, it's possible to secure a large gathering of people. I would rather one person follow me to heaven because of my example than lead 15 million people to hell because of my compromise. If you let God's Word stick to your heart like superglue, than you won't fall prey to dangerous doctrines.

Some of the Pharisees put heavy religious loads on people, and then never offered any assistance. I would rather be a load bearer than a dump truck any day.

David said, "Blessed be the Lord who daily bears our burdens!"(Psalm 68:19). I want to be a load bearer for other people, and when it gets too heavy for me to carry, I know someone with big enough shoulders to bring it to. God never intended for us to go through life struggling to make it on our own merits. That is why He sent His Son. Think of it this way. God cast His Son to earth like a life preserver being tossed in a tumultuous sea. He saw us drowning in our own self-made mess and sent His Son to be our platform (or cornerstone). It was Him that we despised, rejected, and crucified, but in the midst of our ignorance Jesus threw us a lifeline. He said, "Father, forgive them, because they don't know what they are doing"

(Luke 23:34). If you are away from God, come to your senses and grab hold of Jesus with all of your strength so God can pull you to safety.

There is nothing worse than an unused life preserver when you are in a sea of drowning people. It's time to get your life preserver out of the case and begin tossing it out into the vast sea of lost souls.

More Than Just a Building

I believe that the Holy Ghost-filled church is the most powerful force on the earth to bring about radical change in our world. There is not another organization on the planet that wields the influence the church does. It is still the lifeline to the lost and the life preserver to the sinking. God has given His church every tool it needs to accomplish His will on the earth. We are like a good survival knife. We have everything we need, but if we don't use what we have we become rusty.

The church has gone through so much persecution and has still survived every onslaught of the enemy to try to destroy it. The church was not just meant to survive, but to thrive!!

So many people feel as if they don't measure up, or even that it is impossible for God to use them. It is impossible to live a life of victory when you constantly feel that you don't measure up.

There is nothing worse than an unused life preserver when you are in a sea of drowning people.

The Bible says, in 2 Corinthians 6:15: "And what accord has Christ with Belial? Or what part has a believer with an unbeliever?" Christ means anointed One, but Belial means worthlessness. There is a Spirit attached to feeling worthless, but the anointing (anointed One) has come to set you free from discouragement and doubt. He has come to empower you to live an effective, fruitful life!

God has called us all to be lifesavers, but you have to be willing to get close enough to other people who are drowning.

To empower someone means to authorize, to enable, or permit. Can I give you some good news? God has authorized you by His blood, enabled you by His Spirit, and permitted you by His perfect will to live a life of fire and reach nations for His glory.

Acts 1:8 says, "And you shall receive power after that the Holy Ghost has come upon you, and you shall be witnesses of Me in Jerusalem, Judea, Samaria, and the uttermost parts of the earth" (paraphrased).

Second Timothy 1:6-9 (ESV) gives us a perfect picture of a spiritual father empowering his spiritual son:

> 6 For this reason I remind you to fan into flame the gift
> of God, which is in you through the laying on of my
> hands, 7 for God gave us a spirit not of fear but of power
> and love and self-control.
>
> 8 Therefore do not be ashamed of the testimony about
> our Lord, nor of me his prisoner, but share in suffering
> for the gospel by the power of God, 9 who saved us and
> called us to a holy calling, not because of our works but
> because of his own purpose and grace, which he gave us
> in Christ Jesus before the ages began.

We all need people like Paul in our lives who believe in us when nobody else does and who see potential when everybody else sees our problems. God has called us all to be lifesavers, but you have to be willing to get close enough to other people who are drowning. Sometimes that means putting yourself in harm's way.

Chapter 12

Don't Miss It!

Leonard Ravenhill said, "The opportunity of a lifetime must be seized in the lifetime of the opportunity."[34] It's good for us that our gracious God presents us with innumerable opportunities to advance His Kingdom. Where opportunities differ and become unique is in the person, place, and time.

As long as we live, there will always be someone who not only needs to hear the Good News, but is also ready to receive the Good News. Therefore we can never use the excuse that God is through with us.

How many opportunities have you missed because you were waiting for something bigger and better to come along? Because of this attitude we miss out on God doing really big things in our life.

In Acts 3:1-9 (ESV) we read about a lame man that was laid daily at the Gate called Beautiful:

> [1] Now Peter and John were going up to the temple at
> the hour of prayer, the ninth hour. [2] And a man lame

[34] "Quotes," Leonard Ravenhill, http://www.leonard-ravenhill.com/quotes.

> from birth was being carried, whom they laid daily at the gate of the temple that is called the Beautiful Gate to ask alms of those entering the temple. [3] Seeing Peter and John about to go into the temple, he asked to receive alms. [4] And Peter directed his gaze at him, as did John, and said, "Look at us." [5] And he fixed his attention on them, expecting to receive something from them. [6] But Peter said, "I have no silver and gold, but what I do have I give to you. In the name of Jesus Christ of Nazareth, rise up and walk!" [7] And he took him by the right hand and raised him up, and immediately his feet and ankles were made strong. [8] And leaping up he stood and began to walk, and entered the temple with them, walking and leaping and praising God. [9] And all the people saw him walking and praising God.

He was in the right place, at the right time, asking the wrong questions to the right people. He was asking for money and received a miracle. I wonder if he had not asked for money if the disciples would have paid any attention to him. The disciples could have thought that praying for this man was a waste of time just because he was "that lame guy" they passed every day. They could have thought, "What good will this do if we stop and pray?"

God was not drawn to this man just because he was needy. He didn't remove his plight just because he was in distress. What He does do is respond to those who call out to Him. I believe this man's plea for help reached the right ears, not just any ears. Five thousand souls were eventually saved because of seeing this one miracle.

I liken this guy to blind Bartimaeus. Jesus was in the process of passing Bartimaeus, but Bartimaeus stopped him by saying, "Jesus, son of David, have mercy on me!" (Matthew 9:27). He received his sight because he asked the right question, at the right time, to the right person. Unfortunately, sometimes, we who have sight are less perceptive then those who are blind.

We miss prime opportunities because we don't see what the potential outcome of obedience could be. That is why our objective in being obedient should never hinge solely on seeing a grand outcome. Our obedience should always be linked to our relationship with Jesus. Jesus said, "If you love Me, keep my commandments" (John 14:15).

We miss prime opportunities because we don't see what the potential outcome of obedience could be.

God does not want us to miss out on big opportunities just because we think they are too small to waste our time on. In Acts 9:32-35, the Bible tells us a story about Peter praying for a paralytic and the man being healed. It's one of those stories that's easy to miss because it is sandwiched between the story of Paul's conversion and God raising Dorcas from the dead. The magnitude of what happened in this story is amazing.

He prays for a man by the name of Aeneas that was bedridden for eight years, he is healed, and as a result of this healing, verse 35 says "all the residents of Lydda and Sharon turned to the Lord." This is two whole towns caught up in a whirlwind of mass conversions because of one man being healed! WOW! What if Peter would have said, "This is a waste of my time to stop and pray for this man"? He could have sent somebody else out to pray for him, but I think the right time would have passed to see such a magnificent move of God.

We must have a personal redefinition of what it means to be great in the eyes of the Lord. Jesus left the ninety-nine to go after the one lost sheep. He taught the crowds tough lessons, knowing that they would leave Him. The Father cared more about the estranged prodigal son coming home than He did about all the possessions in His house. Do you care more about having a big following, or following in the footsteps of Jesus? Would you leave all your possessions behind to reach your generation?

God can supernaturally enable us with the right gifts in an instant, but will never force us to walk in maturity.

Some people want God to help expand their reach, only to ditch Him later for more popularity. Have you prayed for a big ministry and wondered why God never gave it to you? I know I have. God does not want to set us up for failure. He cares more about our character being bigger than our charisma. Some of us have the passion and experience needed to reach multitudes of people. Unfortunately, the spiritual integrity necessary to accomplish such a work may be decades away from being ready.

Remember, God can supernaturally enable us with the right gifts in an instant, but will never force us to walk in maturity.

Comparisons vs. Compatibility

Many of us have people we look up to, some of which we even try to emulate. When I was a kid I used to tie a towel around my neck and pretend it was my cape. It was easy to go from being a wimpy little kid to superhero status just by changing into a costume. Even though my costume made me feel invincible, underneath the outfit I was still the same old me, but with a boost of confidence.

As we get older, we still do the same thing…we make believe we are something different than what we are. Eve was deceived into thinking she could be different and somehow better than how God originally made her. She compared what she did not have to what she had and determined within herself that she had been cheated out of greatness by God.

Whether we realize it or not, we do the same thing when we compare ourselves to other people. Some comparisons are unreasonable. I would never compare my basketball skills to Shaquille O'Neal's. I am a half an inch shy of six feet tall. He's over seven feet tall. There is nothing I can do to get any taller.

It is this unhealthy dissatisfaction that drives many, especially in the American church. We are enamored by visions of overnight success. We are captivated by the superstars of Christian TV. We beg God to give us the nations, but won't talk to our unsaved friends about the Lord.

I encourage you to pray for the nations, but do not forget about your friends. Dream big, but be willing to start small. Do not envy and covet what some other minister has just because you are not seeing the results they are. Their life could very well be in shambles because of their success.

Second Corinthians 10:12 gives us this warning, "For we dare not make ourselves of the number, or compare ourselves with some that commend themselves: but they measuring themselves by themselves, and comparing themselves among themselves, are not wise" (KJV). God is not looking for copycats; He created us for compatibility with Him. It is only as we gaze into His fiery eyes that our lustful eyes will be purified.

I encourage you to pray for the nations, but do not forget about your friends. Dream big, but be willing to start small.

Through Jesus, God became a man to help restore our identity. He showed us in His earthly life how to connect with His divine nature. Before Jesus came, a curtain separated us from God's holiness. It was a constant reminder of sin's damaging effect on our personal relationship with Him. A sacred covenant and union had been broken. We were no longer compatible with our Creator.

Even though the enemy tried to erase God's indelible fingerprints from our spiritual DNA, Christ transformed the relationship. He did not just fix what we broke, but He made an even better covenant with us. He restored our compatibility with Him by taking up residence in us through His Holy Spirit.

Passion vs. Burden

What is the difference between passion and burden? A passion is something that can come and go, but a burden remains until there is a breakthrough or death. Jesus came to seek and save those which were lost. This wasn't just His passion, or mantra; it was His mission. He died seeing that vision come to pass.

I've found that great men and women of God aren't made that way just because they had passion or a big ministry, but because they were willing to give their life, family, finances, and future to the calling of God. Paul said in Romans chapter 9 that he would be accursed from Christ and give up his own salvation to see the nation of Israel saved. How many of us would lay down our eternal reward in heaven for someone else? We would probably say this was a foolish prayer.

Paul had a burden that he couldn't shake. He admitted that he wasn't even worthy to be called an apostle because he persecuted the church so badly. God had forgiven him of a great debt and now he poured his life out in service to the Lord. He even told Timothy in 2 Timothy 4:6-8:

> [6] For I am already being poured out as a drink offering, and the time of my departure has come. [7] I have fought the good fight, I have finished the race, I have kept the faith. [8] Henceforth there is laid up for me the crown of righteousness, which the Lord, the righteous judge, will award to me on that Day, and not only to me but also to all who have loved his appearing.

These were the words of a man that lived his life in the Lord with no regret!

Oh Lord, Burden Us!

Peter was a man with a burden. Men filled with a heavenly burden are dangerous to the kingdom of darkness. They take courage when other men would cower. They see potential when other men see plight. They are not moved by false fears and vain imaginations. They are not bound by unruly sins and weak convictions. They are strong in the power of His might. We need to take ownership of our responsibility in the great plan of redemption. Those in the church who have remained unmoved by the sinfulness of man have never really come into contact with the holiness of God. We need a burden to carry out His mission on earth. We need a burden to help carry others' burdens.

Men filled with a heavenly burden are dangerous to the kingdom of darkness.

I found a story called "Burden of My Own" that I would like to share:

> A monarch of long ago had twin sons. As they grew to young manhood, the king sought a fair way to designate one of them as crown prince. All who knew the young men thought them equal in intelligence, wit, personal charm, health, and physical strength. Being a keenly observant king, he thought he detected a trait in one which was not shared by the other.
>
> Calling them to his council chamber one day, he said, "My sons, the day will come when one of you must succeed me as king. The weight of sovereignty is very heavy. To find out which of you is better able to bear them cheerfully, I am sending you together to a far corner of the kingdom.
>
> One of my advisors there will place equal burdens on your shoulders. My crown will one day go to the one who first returns bearing his yoke like a king should."
>
> In a spirit of friendly competition, the brothers set out together. Soon they overtook an aged woman struggling under a burden that seemed far too heavy for her frail body. One of the boys suggested that they stop to help

her. The other protested: "We have a saddle of our own to worry about. Let us be on our way."

The objector hurried on while the other stayed behind to give aid to the aged woman. Along the road, from day to day, he found others who also needed help. A blind man took him miles out of his way, and a lame man slowed him to a cripple's walk.

Eventually he did reach his father's advisor, where he secured his own yoke and started home with it safely on his shoulders. When he arrived at the palace, his brother met him at the gate, and greeted him with dismay. He said, "I don't understand. I told our father the weight was too heavy to carry. However did you do it?"

The future king replied thoughtfully, "I suppose when I helped others carry their yoke, I found the strength to carry my own."[35]

Maybe the key to renewed strength is in finding someone else who is suffering under a heavy load and helping them. Mother Teresa would care for people in leper colonies even though leprosy is highly contagious. She was moved by a burden to help hurting people. As we take the role of a "good Samaritan," God will take His role in our lives as the Good Shepherd.

It is a shame when good men do nothing, but it is an even greater shame when Christian men are passive.

What have you given lately? Burden and compassion cause us to step outside our area of lax living and into a life of demonstration. Jesus acted out of compassion when He healed the crowds. He was moved with compassion when He fed the multitudes with the bread and fish. His heart was tender toward the poor

[35] "Burden of My Own",inspiring-quotes-and-stories.com, http://www.inspiring-quotes-and-stories.com/burden.html.

and hurting. He wept when His friend Lazarus died. He laments over the condition of the human heart. It is a shame when good men do nothing, but it is an even greater shame when Christian men are passive. Passion is good, but a burden from the Lord is better.

Find what burdens the Lord and allow it to burden you.

It was because of a burden for the people of Israel that Moses interceded for them so that the Lord would not wipe them out after their rebellion. It was because of Paul's burden for Israel that he wished himself cut off from the salvation of the Lord if it meant that they would inherit salvation. Israel is the apple of God's eye, so it makes sense that He would raise up men and women with a burden to see them saved. If Israel is the apple of His eye, then we dare not mess with them lest we be found poking God in the eye. Find what burdens the Lord and allow it to burden you.

Reinhard Bonnke, an evangelist to the continent of Africa, was given a burden from the Lord that "Africa shall be saved."[36] He took that to heart and devoted his life to work in a place that was known for being a missionary graveyard. He is reaping an amazing harvest of souls, partly due to those who have gone before. Reformer John Knox prayed, "Give me Scotland or I die!"[37] No wonder Mary Queen of Scots declared that she was more afraid of the prayers of John Knox than of an army of ten thousand![38] John Wesley, George Whitefield, Jonathan Edwards, Jeremiah Lamphier, Charles Spurgeon, and many more throughout the years have burned with heavenly burdens.

---

[36] Reinhard Bonnke, Christ for all Nations.

[37] A John Knox prayer heard by his friends as he agonized in prayer for Scotland. *Steve Holt Online;* "Give Me Scotland," http://steveholtonline.org/give-me-scotland/.

[38] Ibid.

The more we linger in His glory, the more we will carry His burden. The word glory literally means weightiness.

Leave a Legacy

Each and every person will have a chance to leave behind a legacy for future generations. Unfortunately, most people end their lives full of regret. They wish they had more time, or worse, they plan their whole existence around what they want and don't even give God the time of day.

Jesus warned us in Matthew 6:19-21 (ESV):

> [19] Do not lay up for yourselves treasures on earth, where moth and rust destroy and where thieves break in and steal, [20] but lay up for yourselves treasures in heaven, where neither moth nor rust destroys and where thieves do not break in and steal. [21] For where your treasure is, there your heart will be also.

Don't miss out on a potential move of God because the timing is not convenient for you. God uses small meetings to bring about huge change. Your greatest moment of promotion in the Lord may just be the moment you least expect.

Your greatest moment of promotion in the Lord may just be the moment you least expect.

One of the most life-altering meetings I have ever had came about when I least expected it. It happened about four years ago in a small town in Indiana. My wife and I were interim youth pastors in Illinois. We knew that God was getting ready to transition us, but we just did not know where or when. I had learned from waiting on God before that He did not always do things within my time frame. I had also learned that it was not good to try to force something to happen prematurely. So we waited "somewhat" patiently for the right door to open up.

In the meantime, we had a church wanting us to come try out for a youth pastor position. The pay was good and they were also offering free housing. It seemed like a great idea, but we did not have a peace about it, so we kept our options open. Around the same time, our worship pastor had moved to Indiana to help his former youth pastor start a church. One weekend he invited us to Indiana to celebrate his wife's birthday. We went out to eat that day and visited his church that night. Later that month we visited again and heard the pastor speak.

God's timing is perfect. The more we learn how to set our watches by His time, the more supernatural encounters we will experience.

I immediately connected with his vision. During the altar ministry he approached me and began praying for me and speaking into my life. He then asked me if I could pray for him. As I did, I felt a rush of the Holy Spirit and I began to pray and prophesy over him. Even though it was my first time meeting him, I could sense an immediate connection. We asked him if he needed any more help in the church. He did. So we put our house on the market to sell and it sold within a month. We moved to Indiana by faith and God supplied for us even through some very lean times.

I would not trade that time in my life for anything. The spiritual lessons I learned were priceless. I am sure that I am who I am today, in part, because of that specific connection. Not to mention, I gained some very close friends in whom I am sure to stay in contact with for the rest of my life. God's timing is perfect. The more we learn how to set our watches by His time, the more supernatural encounters we will experience.

Every day of the Apostle Paul's life was lived according to God's calendar. He was not always an apostle. Before he met Jesus on the road to Damascus he thought he was living with God's best interest in mind. He called himself zealous, and he considered himself to be a Pharisee of Pharisees. He thought he was fulfilling his ultimate purpose, but later realized he was robbing Jesus of His beautiful bride.

On the road to Damascus, Jesus redirected his misguided zeal and set his life in a whole new direction. Now he lived his life with a Kingdom purpose in the light of eternity. No longer was he a stumbling block to those of the Way; he now became a stepping-stone for the Gentiles.

His writings are considered to be unmatched by any other New Testament writer. Having studied under the great Gamaliel, he wrote with much attention to detail concerning the Torah; but now through inspiration of the Holy Spirit his understanding came alive. He went to his executioners having finished his race. But before he made this final missionary journey, he left his spiritual son, Timothy, with these penetrating words:

Second Timothy 4:1-2 (ESV):

> [1] I charge you in the presence of God and of Christ Jesus, who is to judge the living and the dead, and by his appearing and his kingdom: [2] preach the word; be ready in season and out of season; reprove, rebuke, and exhort, with complete patience and teaching.

May these words resonate in your heart and motivate you to undivided service to the Lord.

Chapter 13

The Grace Awakening

—⁓—

I remember my first trip to the ocean. It was amazing! I stood on the edge of the sandy bank in Myrtle Beach, South Carolina, mesmerized by the vastness of the sea. For hours I paused and listened to the tranquil sounds of the water crashing against the shore. When you are a rowdy, rambunctious ten-year-old it takes something pretty awesome to stop you dead in your tracks. The beautiful horizon seemed close enough to touch. The sun perching on top of the water resembled a huge orange balloon floating in the distance.

I loved watching the surfers ride the big waves. They seemed, if it were possible, to glide across the waves like one would glide down a Slip 'N Slide®. I knew how to swim in a swimming pool with minimal difficulty, so I thought swimming in the ocean would be a piece of cake. I was terribly mistaken. The tide was too strong and I was nearly swept out into the salty abyss before I knew what hit me.

Many people feel that way in life. They set out on an adventure, not realizing the pitfalls, and they end up washed back ashore miles from their destination. Unfortunately, Christians experience the same thing, and oftentimes the outcome can be even more devastating for them because they assume God has their back in every misadventure they try.

They operate outside the grace of God. They plan their own way and then ask God to bless it. Instead of success they are met with failure; and instead of accepting they messed up, they accuse God of letting them fall on their face. Trust me; I have had my fair share of face-plants over the years!

Let me assure you that God's grace is still amazing. It is not only a grace that saves; it is also a grace that sustains. My prayer is by the end of this chapter you will have a "grace awakening."

Kneading Grace

One of my favorite pastimes is baking. There is nothing like the sweet-smelling aroma of bread baking away in the oven. Growing up, we used to have a wood stove in an old farmhouse. My mom would let bread rise on the stove all day long. For hours the fragrance of the bread would fill the house, resulting in a sensory overload. My mouth is watering just thinking about it.

Jesus did not come to condemn you, but to embrace you.

The thought of God's amazing grace should fill our very being. When we fall, there should not be a looming cloud of condemnation that follows us around. Instead there should be an immediate recognition of our sin, which leads to heartfelt repentance. Jesus did not come to condemn you, but to embrace you.

I can imagine grace working in us much like a baker would knead dough. If you work the dough too much you will be left with tough bread. If you work it too little the lump of dough will not take proper form. Who decides how well grace works? You do. Colossians 3:15-17 (ESV) says:

> 15 And let the peace of Christ rule in your hearts, to
> which indeed you were called in one body. And be

> thankful. [16] Let the word of Christ dwell in you richly, teaching and admonishing one another in all wisdom, singing psalms and hymns and spiritual songs, with thankfulness in your hearts to God. [17] And whatever you do, in word or deed, do everything in the name of the Lord Jesus, giving thanks to God the Father through him.

Grace is only good to those who receive it and live within its God-given mandates.

It is easy to have a works mentality. We love to overcomplicate our position before God. The Lord takes delight in being with us. He is a holy God that abhors sin, but also a loving God who adores relationship. Forgiveness is the great equalizer. It has rescued me from discouragement, clothed me with righteousness, and ushered me into the presence of God time and time again. There is a bumper sticker that says "I'm not perfect, just forgiven." This should be our motto.

Grace is only good to those who receive it and live within its God-given mandates. Grace is a covenant. The term covenant is of Latin origin (*con venire*), meaning a coming together. The general meaning of covenant in the Old Testament is bond. It refers to two or more parties bound together. You made a covenant with grace when you turned away from your sinful life to walk in newness of life. You made an eternal exchange. Jesus made it very clear what kind of commitment He expects from us.

On the other hand, grace does not and will not excuse ongoing sin. It confronts sin by enabling us to live above it. Grace empowers us to say no to sin and yes to God. Romans 6:1-2 says, "What shall we say then? Shall we continue in sin, that grace may abound? God forbid. How shall we, that are dead to sin, live any longer therein?" Grace is not our license to do whatever we want.

Grace Under Fire

When I was twenty-five, I started courting my wife. Within a few months I had already made up my mind to ask her to marry me. I knew this meant getting her a ring. I saved every dollar I could, which was not an easy task because I worked as a waiter at a country club. Every time we were out shopping I would sneak off to a jewelry store to spy out the best ring. The jewelry stores would always keep their rings locked away behind thick glass. No matter where I went they would have different displays, but I never wanted to choose a ring without first examining it up close.

There is definitely a biblically inconsistent grace message that has crept into the church. The propagators of this teaching offer a nice display case, but upon closer inspection their "grace" message is polluted. God looks over His Word to perform it. He is not obligated to bless our interpretation of His Word. Acts 14:3 says, "So they remained for a long time, speaking boldly for the Lord, who bore witness to the word of his grace, granting signs and wonders to be done by their hands" (ESV). The message of grace originated with God. Man did not think of it, so why are they spending so much time trying to redefine its meaning?

Many of these teachers preach that God has forgiven all sins: past, present, and future. Some have even gone as far as disregarding all Scripture before the cross, saying it's no longer necessary due to the new covenant. This is in direct contradiction to Scripture. Second Timothy 3:15-17 says,

> [15] and how from childhood you have been acquainted with the sacred writings, which are able to make you wise for salvation through faith in Christ Jesus. [16] All Scripture is breathed out by God and profitable for teaching, for reproof, for correction, and for training in righteousness, [17] that the man of God may be complete, equipped for every good work.

The Bible builds us a great framework in which to view grace. Titus 2:11-12 says, "For the grace of God has appeared, bringing salvation to all men, instructing us to deny ungodliness and worldly desires and to live sensibly, righteously and godly in the present age." I want to expound on the bounty of truths that can be drawn from this passage.

1. Grace is here. It does not have to be worked up. It is not magical, or mystical. It is not ethereal. It is eternal. It existed in God and has been made manifest to all men. It is not bound by time, or space. As a believer, I should be able to access grace no matter where I am.

2. Grace offers the greatest gift of all. It brings salvation to everyone who is ready to receive. It is like receiving a gift from your mom. Mom did not always give me what I wanted, but she always knew what I needed.

3. Grace comes with instructions. God has given us some wonderful instructions: His commandments. They are not in competition with grace, as many have taught, but in fact are in perfect harmony with the message of grace. Only through grace can we have a proper perspective of His commandments. Have you ever tried to put something together without instructions? It is awful. It does not matter if it is a kid's toy or the Taj Mahal; without blueprints it is nearly impossible. Good thing God is a master architect, having framed the world with just His words. He knows how to design a blueprint. In this verse His blueprint is easy to understand. He does not mince words, but with pristine clarity states what grace requires of us. Grace does not ask too much of us.

4. Grace is current. It helps in this present age. This generation is crying out for grace and acceptance. Like generations gone by, they long for understanding. All cultural differences aside, they want a real display of grace. If they don't see us "denying ungodliness and worldly desires"

they will assume nothing is required of them. We lead by example. Immaturity will never reproduce maturity.

Great Grace

We need to transition from cheap grace to great grace. Acts 4:33 says, "And with great power gave the apostles witness of the resurrection of the Lord Jesus: and great grace was upon them all" (KJV). I want to draw another perspective than my own from an excerpt taken from a message preached by Smith Wigglesworth on October 31, 1922:

> "And great grace was upon them all." Great grace is upon us when we magnify the Lord. If ever you want to see what God means when He gets a chance at His people, have a peep at the fourth chapter of Acts, and see what God did. Just because all the people shouted aloud to Him He imparted to them such blessing that every person was filled with the Holy Ghost, and I believe what God wants to do in these days is to give an inward manifestation of His divine presence within the body until the body is moved by the power of the Spirit. Beloved, we are accustomed to earthly things, but when God sends the heavenly it is beyond our understanding. Oh, to have the revelation of the mind of God! It fills my soul, the thought of it! Oh, for the kind of loosening of the body that we will never be bound again! Just filled with God!
>
> I believe God wants us to understand something of the words of this life. What life? The manifestation of the power of Jesus in the human body, a divine life, a divine power, a quickening, thrilling energy given to you. I was baptized with the Holy Ghost in 1907. If anyone had said to me: "Now, Wigglesworth, you will see such and such things," it would have been beyond my human comprehension, but the tide has risen for fifteen years,

> and it is still rising. Thank God, there has never been a black day, nor a blank day.
>
> When I think about the first Church, how God favored her, how He burst thru her, how He definitely spoke, how He transformed Christians and made them move with the power of apostles, that wherever they went they transformed lives—God did such wonderful things, and when I think of it, I think, that we should have something far in advance, and say: "Look up; your redemption draweth nigh!" I want to take a perspective of what they were, and we must be. I am inwardly convinced of the power that awaits us, the installation of God's movement right in our hearts.[39]

God longs to grant His church with great grace, but can we be trusted with such awesome favor as the early church enjoyed? Salvation is free to us, but trust comes at a cost.

Grace to Grow

Did you know we are supposed to grow in grace? Second Peter 3:18 says, "But grow in grace, and in the knowledge of our Lord and Saviour Jesus Christ. To him be glory both now and forever. Amen" (KJV). We have a choice to accept this process, or decline it.

Sanctification is not instant. It is a process. Grace was given so we could navigate through this process with greater ease. The body needs proper nourishment. This includes having the right amount of protein. Many people suffer with protein deficiency. Some symptoms of protein deficiency are: constant cravings, muscle or joint pain, lack of sleep, and low energy, which can lead to stress.

[39] "Great Grace Upon the Church". smithwigglesworth.com, http://www.smithwigglesworth.com/sermons/misc10.htm. Excerpt from the message preached at Pentecostal Union Meeting, Chicago, October 31, 1922.

We show many of the same symptoms when we lack grace.

1. **Constant Cravings:** We crave attention from everyone around us. We make up for our spiritual lack by seeking man's approval. A lack of grace can make us feel that God is distant and uninterested. King David had an amazing revelation of the nearness of God.

In Psalm 139:1-18 (NKJV) he says,

[1] "O Lord, You have searched me and known *me.*
[2] You know my sitting down and my rising up;
You understand my thought afar off.
[3] You comprehend my path and my lying down,
And are acquainted with all my ways.
[4] For *there is* not a word on my tongue,
But behold, O Lord, You know it altogether.
[5] You have hedged me behind and before,
And laid Your hand upon me.
[6] *Such* knowledge *is* too wonderful for me;
It is high, I cannot *attain* it.

[7] Where can I go from Your Spirit?
Or where can I flee from Your presence?
[8] If I ascend into heaven, You *are* there;
If I make my bed in hell, behold, You *are there.*
[9] *If* I take the wings of the morning,
And dwell in the uttermost parts of the sea,
[10] Even there Your hand shall lead me,
And Your right hand shall hold me.
[11] If I say, "Surely the darkness shall fall on me,"
Even the night shall be light about me;
[12] Indeed, the darkness shall not hide from You,
But the night shines as the day;
The darkness and the light *are* both alike *to You.*

[13] For You formed my inward parts;
You covered me in my mother's womb.
[14] I will praise You, for I am fearfully *and* wonderfully made;

Marvelous are Your works,
And *that* my soul knows very well.
15 My frame was not hidden from You,
When I was made in secret,
And skillfully wrought in the lowest parts of the earth.
16 Your eyes saw my substance, being yet unformed.
And in Your book they all were written,
The days fashioned for me,
When *as yet there were* none of them.

17 How precious also are Your thoughts to me, O God!
How great is the sum of them!
18 *If* I should count them, they would be more in number than the sand;
When I awake, I am still with You.

2. **Muscle and joint pain:** Grace is like lubricant to our joints. Ephesians 4:15-16 says, "but speaking the truth in love, we are to grow up in all aspects into Him who is the head, even Christ, from whom the whole body, being fitted and held together by what every joint supplies, according to the proper working for each individual part, causes the growth of the body for the building up of itself in love." This verse shows us that the body grows and is built up by love. Love embodies grace. It is the container by which grace is expressed to others. An abusive, backbiting church has a grace deficiency. A church full of contention and dissension has a grace deficiency. Remember, love covers a multitude of sins. How we treat others will eventually reciprocate back on us.

3. **Loss of sleep:** People who remain outside the grace of God never fully come to a place of rest. In Matthew 11:28, rest is given to those who "come to the Lord." Many are sick in body today because they refuse to apply the fourth commandment to their life. Exodus 20:8 says, "Remember the Sabbath day by keeping it holy." The Israelites never came to a place of rest in the Promised

Land. The wilderness was only supposed to take a few days to cross. The Promised Land is where they were meant to live blessed lives, and then die peacefully. The God of Grace was meant to be their place of refuge. Many of them wanted their bondage in Egypt over their blessings in the Promised Land. We do the same thing today. We brag about our past lifestyle and complain about our new life. We ask God to take us to the next level, even though we have barely learned how to crawl. The author of Hebrews gives us this wonderful promise: "There remains therefore a rest for the people of God" (Hebrews 4:9).

4. **Low energy:** Wherever there is a deficiency of grace, there will always be an unsettling sense of insufficiency. This leads to stress. Your physical and spiritual strength will drain, your senses will become dull, and your frustration will peak. Allow me to add a little side note: just because someone is under the canopy of God's grace does not exclude them from experiencing setbacks. Paul was instructed by the Lord to go to Jerusalem, even though Agabus prophesied about his imprisonment. Once he was even stoned, then thrown out of the city and raised by the prayers of the disciples. Talk about a stressful day. Only God's grace could have given him the strength to overcome.

The Treasure of Grace

Second Corinthians 4:6-7 says, "For God, who said, 'Light shall shine out of darkness,' is the One who has shone in our hearts to give the Light of the knowledge of the glory of God in the face of Christ. But we have this treasure in earthen vessels, so that the surpassing greatness of the power will be of God and not from ourselves."

Whether you believe it or not, you are the crowning achievement of God's creation. He treasures you for you! No other creature has the privilege of hosting His presence like we do. This is an incredible thought considering how flawed we are.

He treasures you for you! No other creature has the privilege of hosting His presence like we do.

Last year, I heard a story of a Nigerian sailor by the name of Harrison Okene. At the age of twenty-nine, he was stuck underwater for three days after heavy waves sunk the Chevron oil tugboat he was on. Harrison was trapped in a compartment of the submerged boat, kept alive by an air pocket that had not filled up with water. He had no food, but by the grace of God, cola cans just happened to be floating all around him. He had an eerie feeling that he was not alone. He knew his dead crewmates had become fish bait. As he sat there surrounded by death and a watery grave, something amazing happened. A rescue diver by the name of Nico van Heerden unknowingly illuminated the small air pocket with his flashlight. Suddenly, out of nowhere, Okene grabbed Nico's hand. He was brought safely to the top of the water and was immediately put in a decompression chamber to help readjust him to the decreased pressure of the atmosphere.

We, much like Okene, were trapped in an unforgiving grave. Before Christ's death on the cross the grave was permanent; and before we experienced His saving grace we were imprisoned by the ice-cold grip of sin. Like a hardened criminal on death row, we were awaiting the long walk down the green mile. We were surrounded by inmates with the unpleasant aroma of death. The only difference is most people do not even know the second death awaits them.

Do you want to know the wonderful news? God's grace has the ability to rewrite your ending. Matthew 26:27-28 records The Lord's Supper: "And when He had taken a cup and given thanks, He gave it to them, saying, 'Drink from it, all of you; for this is My blood of the covenant, which is poured out for many for forgiveness of sins.'" Jesus has shred our spiritual death

Death had its origins with sin, in the first Adam, but the second Adam has come with life.

certificate and is offering us a new birth certificate. Death was never meant to have the final word. Death had its origins with sin, in the first Adam, but the second Adam has come with life.

Jesus has shone His light in our darkened hearts like the rescue diver's flashlight which cut through the murky waters and entered the sunken compartment of the tugboat. Isaiah 9:2 says, "The people that walked in darkness have seen a great light: they that dwell in the land of the shadow of death, upon them hath the light shined" (KJV).

John 1:4-5 says, "In him was life; and the life was the light of men. And the light shineth in darkness; and the darkness comprehended it not" (KJV).

On October 8, 1871, D. L. Moody preached to a capacity crowd at Chicago's Farwell Hall. His message centered on the question Pilate asked the crowd at Jesus' trial. It was entitled, "What shall I do then with Jesus?" The closing of his sermon was interrupted by the sound of fire trucks. Upon seeing the restlessness of the crowd, Moody dismissed the service early with the instructions to go home and think about what he had preached and then come back the next Sabbath to make a decision. Off in the distance billows of smoke and a raging fire consumed the sky. As the winds increased, the flames spread from house to house, incinerating thousands of buildings. By the time it was extinguished, the once bustling city resembled a horrific war zone. In the aftermath of this tragedy Moody said;

> "I have never seen that congregation since, and I never will meet those people again until I meet them in another world. But I want to tell you of one lesson I learned that night, which I have never forgotten, and that is, when I preach, to press Christ upon the people then and there

> and try to bring them to a decision on the spot…I have asked God many times to forgive me for telling people that night to take a week to think it over."[40]

It is the steadfast mercy of God that affords men countless opportunities to surrender to His saving grace. A raging tempest is a brew which threatens to destroy the souls of men. To capture the heart of a reluctant generation we must introduce them to a God of grace. God has chosen us to be the vessels through which this pure message must be imparted.

[40] "D. L. Moody's Story," http://www.moody.edu/DL-moody/. Quote, 1893; twenty-two years after the Chicago Fire.

Darrin and Eva Vaughan

About the Author

Darrin Vaughan is a powerful speaker, author, and the founder of Darrin Vaughan Ministries. Darrin has been married to his wife, Eva since 2006. He and Eva have a *vision* to reach those who have not yet experienced the saving grace of Jesus Christ, and to equip leaders who are fervent in their pursuit of God and authentic in their love for humanity.

After receiving salvation at the age of seventeen, Darrin was ready to grow in his relationship with the Lord. He knew God was calling him to surrender his life completely. He began serving his church in whatever area was needed. Darrin's pastor noticed his zeal and offered to mentor him.

Around the age of twenty-two, Darrin obtained his ministry credentials through Global University of the Assemblies of God. He later attended Master's Commission, where he received in-depth discipleship training in church ministry and outreach evangelism. Darrin has preached at various church services and youth camps in the United States and has also served in leadership as an associate pastor, student ministry pastor, and co-church planter.

In 2010, Darrin started working for Christ for all Nations, the ministry of evangelists Reinhard Bonnke and Daniel Kolenda. Darrin has had the opportunity to travel to Africa, assist with large evangelistic meetings, and help mobilize leaders for the Reinhard Bonnke Gospel Campaigns (cfan.org and gospelcrusade.org).

Several years ago, God began stirring Darrin's heart to see the lost and hurting find grace, forgiveness, and hope through the love of the Father. As Darrin spent time in prayer and preparation, God was giving him a burden to reach a generation. His passion compelled him to start Darrin Vaughan Ministries as a way to spread the Good News of Jesus through resources, outreach, missions, and other ministry projects. Darrin believes in connecting with other pastors, leaders, churches, and ministries for the purpose of building up, equipping, and sending out.

If you would like to connect with Darrin Vaughan, or to schedule Darrin for a church service, conference, camp, or outreach, please email info@darrinvaughan.com.

darrinvaughan.com

www.ingramcontent.com/pod-product-compliance
Lightning Source LLC
LaVergne TN
LVHW052026080426
835513LV00018B/2184
* 9 7 8 0 6 9 2 0 2 5 0 1 7 *